Mary Connell,

When doesn't a mi-

make you/me/anyone feel better?

Happy Shower!

Love, Francine

Thoroughly Modern Milkshakes

THOROUGHLY MODERN
MILKSHAKES

Adam Ried

Photographs by André Baranowski

W. W. NORTON & COMPANY   NEW YORK   LONDON

Also by Adam Ried

Williams-Sonoma New Flavors for Soups

For information about permission to reproduce selections from this book,
write to Permissions, W. W. Norton & Company, Inc.,
500 Fifth Avenue, New York, NY 10110

For information about special discounts for bulk purchases, please contact
W. W. Norton Special Sales at specialsales@wwnorton.com or 800-233-4830

Manufacturing by Worzalla
Book design by Wesley Gott
Production manager: Julia Druskin

Library of Congress Cataloging-in-Publication Data

Ried, Adam.
Thoroughly modern milkshakes / Adam Ried ; photographs by Andre
Baranowski.—1st ed.
p. cm.
Includes index.
ISBN 978-0-393-06877-1 (hardcover)
1. Milkshakes. I. Title.
TX817.M5R54 2009
641.8'75—dc22

2009009073

W. W. Norton & Company, Inc.
500 Fifth Avenue, New York, N.Y. 10110
www.wwnorton.com

W. W. Norton & Company Ltd.
Castle House, 75/76 Wells Street, London W1T 3QT

1 2 3 4 5 6 7 8 9 0

In memory of my mother and father, Noël and Hal Ried.

ACKNOWLEDGMENTS

Writing a book, even on a topic as frothy as milkshakes, takes some doing, and many people play a hand. I extend a hearty thanks to anyone and everyone who encouraged me, challenged me, pushed or prodded me, inspired me, taught me, and/or tolerated me. In particular:

My esteemed friend and yoga teacher Jarvis Chen, whose sprinkle of cardamom started this whole thing.

My sister, Amanda Hewell, who, admit it or not, leads the culinary charge in our family, and who willingly conspired in a milkshake marathon the likes of which we could not have imagined when we started. By the end, if you had stabbed either one of us, we'd have bled cream. Really, these recipes are as much Amanda's as they are mine.

My brother, Josh Ried, for incisive and enthusiastic counsel on the matter of *batidos* and *licuados*, with which he is intimately familiar from many, many trips to the relevant zones tropicale.

My (now rather scattered) *Cook's Illustrated* and *America's Test Kitchen* families, particularly Pam Anderson, Jack Bishop, Lori Galvin, Eva Katz, Chris Kimball, Amy Klee, India Koopman, Henrietta Murray, Doc Willoughby, and most especially Raquel Pelzel for her wise, generous, and easy-going friendship (and also for squatter's rights during the photo shoot), Kay Rentschler for her rollicking spirit, irrepressible intellect, and all-around electricity, and Dawn Yanagihara, my partner in the faux firm of Arctic, Oblivious, and Fatbag (as we called the blissfully over-air-conditioned room that we shared while working together there), for interest, inspiration, ingenuity, and involvement far above and beyond the call of duty.

My ever-accommodating team at the *Boston Globe Magazine*, Anne Nelson, John Burgess, Brendan Stephens, Jim Scherer, and Catrine Kelty.

My intrepid tasters, testers, friends, and advisers David Bromley, Brian Burke, Paule Caillat, Greg Case, Kathleen Collins, Elizabeth and Jonathan Green, Sherry Meek, Sally Sampson, Mama, Greg(arious) Tasis, and Shinei Tsukamoto.

My equipment providers, Mary Beth Perreault-Dukes at Hamilton Beach, Ilona Gollinger at Waring, Wendy Manfredi at Vitamix, and Jordan Byrnes for Homeland Housewares.

My photography team—André Baranowski, Michael Pederson (an all-out hero, able to scale tall buildings in a single bound and chill shakes with just Styrofoam and dry ice), and Cathy Cook and Paige Hicks, mistresses of glassware, plates, platters, spoons, straws, napkins, fabrics, and more.

My agent, Angela Miller; my editor, Maria Guarnaschelli; and my publishing and design team—Margaret Maloney, Melanie Tortoroli, Rebecca Carlisle, Steve Colca, Ingsu Liu, Julia Druskin, Wesley Gott, Erica Heitman-Ford, Virginia McRae, Polly Mancini, Alexandra Nickerson, Susan Sanfrey, and Nancy Palmquist.

And of course, my partner, Tim Kinnel, the sorbet in the milkshake of my life (read on . . . you'll understand).

CONTENTS

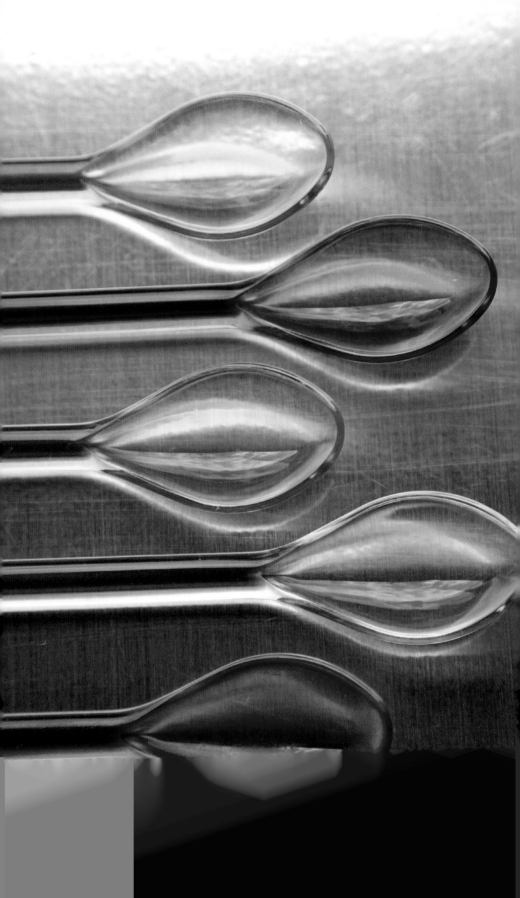

INTRODUCTION

Milkshakes—the sweet, frosty amalgams of ice cream, milk, syrup, and pure joy loved by young and old and everyone in between— are the quintessential old-fashioned treat. They hark back to a simpler time of quaint ice cream parlors, drugstore soda fountains, and Woolworth's lunch counters; of one glass, two straws, and your high school sweetheart.

Scrrrrraaaaaaaaaaaaattttch!!!

Fast forward to 2009, smack-dab in the middle of the computer age. Now we multitask and e-mail and blog through our days. We hyperventilate without wireless Internet access. Cars navigate and park themselves, and our BlackBerries and iPhones *are* the bosses of us.

We've all had to grow up to face the pace and the technology. And if I have to scratch and scrape my way into the twenty-first century, then so too must my shake!! It's prime time to modernize the milkshake.

Don't get me wrong, there is absolutely nothing . . . n-o-t-h-i-n-g . . . wrong with a great, standard-issue chocolate or vanilla shake. Both have served us admirably since the popularization of milkshakes in the 1920s and still do. But for food enthusiasts who are ever more sophisticated, adventurous, well-traveled, and open to innovative ingredients and flavor combinations, plain chocolate or vanilla shakes can be as much a starting point as an end in themselves.

Think of *Thoroughly Modern Milkshakes* as your guide to milkshake modernization. There is really nothing fancy here, just imaginative flavor innovations based on common ingredients, some that have been around for ages and others that are newer to the marketplace. You'll taste how the essence of basil transforms a strawberry shake, how a few grains of smoky chipotle chile powder invigorate a chocolate shake, and how a drizzle of toasty sesame oil and a dab of honey give a whole new twist to a familiar vanilla shake.

The Building Blocks of Milkshake Modernization

Supermarkets, ethnic markets, farmers' markets, and liquor stores offer an arsenal of products for updating and intensifying milkshake flavors. You just have to think outside the lines of the milkshakes you have always known.

Sorbet First and foremost, let me sing the praises of sorbet, which I consider to be *the* key tool in our milkshake revitalization program. Viscous syrups have long served as the primary flavoring agent of shakes, and they have served with honor and distinction. To my taste, though, commercial syrups are generally sweeter than truly flavorful. They just don't offer much depth.

Sorbet, on the other hand, is not as sweet and is much more forcefully flavored. This realization hit home one night over a pint of chocolate sorbet. As I dug my way through, I was struck by the intense flavor of cocoa. Not sugar. Not dairy. Pure, powerful, dark, brooding cocoa. In the name of research I broke out a bottle of chocolate syrup to taste alongside, and there was no comparison. On a flavor scale of 1 to 10, the sorbet was about a 12. The syrup hovered around 6. Naturally, my next step was to make a milkshake with the sorbet—what other reaction could I have had? There was coffee ice cream in the freezer, so a mocha shake it would be. And what a mocha shake it was! Blending the chocolate sorbet with coffee ice cream produced spine-tingling new dimensions in mocha. Balancing the dairy richness of ice cream with more forceful flavors does a milkshake good. I was on to something here.

The same can be said for fruit sorbets. Bright, concentrated fruit flavors, from lemon to mango to raspberry to tangerine, open doors to vibrantly flavored shakes that would leave our grandparents wondering what hit them. Nowadays, sorbet is more common and widely available than syrup—do you know any supermarket that doesn't carry it? And there is no lack of variety when it comes to flavors. For instance, Häagen-Dazs produces chocolate, coconut, mango, peach, raspberry, strawberry, and lemon. Most decently stocked supermarkets will have at least half of these flavors, if not more (my market carries them all). In this selection alone lie milkshake flavor riches.

Choices become even more extensive when you look at the sorbet flavors offered by other brands. In its store brand, 365, Whole Foods Market sells tangerine, hibiscus, passion fruit, pomegranate, Meyer lemon, strawberry, and raspberry sorbets. Ciao Bella Gelato, an East Coast brand out of New York City, produces twenty-six flavors of sorbet. And of course every region has small producers that market their own, often very creative, flavors. Pear-ginger, anyone? Grapefruit-Campari? Blackberry-lime? Green tea–Verbena? Apricot-Chardonnay? Blood orange? Green apple? Champagne? The list goes on. In the old days of drugstore soda fountains, there would be no Chocolate-Tangerine Shake (page 71), no Cantaloupe-Lemon Shake (page 134), but these days sorbet makes such treats possible.

Spices and herbs Up until now, milkshake makers have pretty much ignored spices such as cinnamon, cloves, cardamom, anise, ground dried chiles, and even black pepper, leaving them instead to baking and savory cooking. Likewise fresh herbs like basil, thyme, and tarragon. Yet these ingredients stand ready to impart their distinctive flavors to milkshakes, elevating them from everyday to extraordinary. You need only taste the intriguing, warmly spiced Pain d'Épices Shake (page 165) or the Lemon-Thyme Shake (page 136) or the Mocha-Cardamom Shake (page 97) to see what I mean.

Nuts and seeds, and their butters and oils Nuts are a common ice cream mix-in and an all-important element of a good ice cream sundae, but seldom are they incorporated into a shake. That's a pity, because they offer rich, toasted, beguiling flavors. If the nuts themselves are soft enough, pecans for instance, you can puree them into the shake—think of the Maple–Butter Pecan shake (page 171), where extra toasted nuts boost the gentle nutty flavor of the butter pecan ice cream. Nut butters, such as peanut or cashew (and even chocolate-hazelnut spread, like Nutella), blend even more easily and smoothly, and they make for some unexpected and delicious flavor combinations like the Peanut-Molasses Shake (page 159); the Vanilla, Rum, and Salted Cashew Shake (page 57); and the Gianduja Shake (page 68).

If you cook Asian-inspired dishes, you probably already have a bottle of toasted sesame oil on hand. Go grab it right now and check out the unusual and aromatic Vanilla-Honey-Sesame Shake (page 53) for a startling and scrumptious new angle on plain vanilla.

Cultured dairy products Crème fraîche, sour cream, and buttermilk provide shakes with an embarrassment of riches—silky texture,

A Brief History of the Milkshake

To most everyone who has studied the matter, the milkshake timeline began in 1885, the year in which they were first referred to in print. Considered both a restorative tonic and a treat, at that point milkshakes usually contained milk, ice, sugar, and, by all indications, an egg and a shot of whiskey, and they were shaken by hand.

Developing on a parallel track that dates back to the early 1870s was another health tonic called malted milk. Patented in 1883 by William Horlick and originally conceived as an artificial baby food by William's brother, James, malted milk gained popularity throughout the 1880s and 1890s, transforming along the way from a nutritious drink for the very young (and very old) to a treat appreciated by people of all ages.

It's not clear exactly how and when milkshakes lost their shot of whiskey and merged with malted milk, but it's no surprise that they did. In 1911 malted milkshakes received a boost toward wider distribution and popularity with the invention of the Hamilton Beach Drink Mixer. The mixer was marketed to drugstore soda fountains, which used them to churn out malted milkshakes with more ease and speed than ever before.

A pivotal year for the milkshake was 1922. Two seminal events occurred, one moving the consistency of milkshakes toward the whipped, aerated, frothy drink that we know today, and the other catapulting an already popular drink to even greater glory. First was the invention of the electric blender, widely credited to Steven Poplawski, a Polish immigrant living in Racine, Wisconsin. Though the blender's design would continue to be refined into the next decade, even at its most primitive it was able to whip and aerate milkshakes for a smoother, fluffier consistency, and the public approved.

The second event took place in Chicago, in the summer of 1922. The soda jerk at a Walgreens drugstore soda fountain, a man named Ivar "Pop" Coulson, altered the basic malted milk formula of milk, chocolate syrup, and malt powder by adding vanilla ice cream. Over the next few years, the new malted milkshake became the star attraction at all the soda fountains in the Walgreens chain, which had stores in several major U.S. cities. Newspaper coverage, word of mouth, and lines snaking out of Walgreens doors propelled the shake to national popularity.

Following the arrival of freon-cooled refrigerators in the late 1920s, automated ice cream machines were developed using similar technology. Based on the latest automatic ice cream machines, in 1936 a man named Earl Prince invented the Multimixer, an automatic milkshake machine that produced five shakes at a time, dispensing them into waiting vessels with the pull of a lever.

The serving vessels of choice were paper cups, purchased from a salesman named Ray Kroc. Deeply impressed with the Multimixer, Kroc convinced Earl Prince to sell him the exclusive rights to the machine. Kroc gave up on paper cups; suddenly he was in the milkshake business, selling Multimixers to restaurants and soda fountains across America. With the spread of the Multimixer, the milkshake became more available and popular than ever.

Also during that period, in 1940, the Dairy Queen franchise of soft serve ice cream restaurants was established. By 1950 there were more than 1,400 Dairy Queens, and in 1949 they began serving milkshakes and malts. Yet another step toward mass milkshake distribution.

In 1954, Ray Kroc met two of his biggest customers, Dick and Mac McDonald, brothers who ran a small chain of hamburger stands in California. The McDonalds sold only hamburgers, fries, and milkshakes. That 1954 meeting not only led to the founding of the McDonald's Corporation and the Golden Arches now recognized by most of the world's population, it also contributed to the establishment of the milkshake as the cultural icon it is today.

subtle tang, and earthy notes that can frame sweet flavors in a whole new way. Shakes like the Sweet Guava and Crème Fraîche Shake (page 116), the Date-Buttermilk Shake (page 140), and the Triple Peach–Buttermilk Shake (page 49) show off the tongue-tingling interplay of sweet and tangy.

Liqueurs and spirits

Far beyond the province of cocktails, flavorful liqueurs and bracing, aromatic spirits can subtly amplify other flavors in a milkshake or act as major players themselves, giving the shake a suave, sophisticated presence. For instance, chestnuts have a mild flavor, and the tiny amount of cognac in the Marron Glacé Shake (page 161) magnifies it. Likewise, the small amount of Calvados in the Tarte Tatin Shake (page 163) makes the apple flavor more prominent.

In the Chocolate-Guinness Shake (page 73), the bittersweet, malty stout plays off the deep cocoa flavor of the chocolate sorbet so the two share equal billing. The Caffè Corretto Shake (page 88) also calls upon spirits to balance and add dimension to a primary flavor, in this case coffee.

Of course, there are also some shakes where the liquor is front and center, and the Zabaglione Shake (page 152) is one, showcasing the sweet, spicy, nutty character of the Marsala that flavors it.

Fruit jams, preserves, juice concentrates, and oils

Jams, preserves, and other concentrated fruit products, more than most juices and nectars, constitute a long-overlooked treasure trove of flavor nuance and intrigue just ripe for upgrading milkshakes. Their raison d'être is to capture the essences of the fruits from which they are made, and to impart it to the dishes in which they are used. The Black Forest Shake (page 75) is one beneficiary, receiving an extra shot of cherry flavor from preserves used to back up the cherry-vanilla ice cream. Similarly, strawberry preserves add to the stupendousness of the Stupendous Strawberry Shake (page 45). Orange juice concentrate serves well when you need a bright, sunny, acidic hit of orange, as I did to help define the Orange Blossom and Honey Shake (page 173). Citrus oils convey the aroma and intense flavor of citrus zest as opposed to the fresh, lighter flavor of the juice. In the Malted Orange-Molasses Shake (page 160), orange oil is no shrinking violet in the face of mighty molasses and malt.

Sweet produce Don't overlook the milkshake possibilities at the local farmers' market. Beautiful, fragrant, perfectly ripe apricots and peaches and pears will be great in shakes; just try the Apricot-Amaretto Shake (page 125), the White Peach Melba Shake with Raspberry Granita (page 123), and the Poire William Shake (page 127) for all the evidence you'll need. But would you ever have imagined combining tomatoes with peaches? They make a great summer salad together, and their sweet-tart flavors achieve similar success in the Tomato-Peach Shake (page 122).

Not many people think of milkshakes when they see a bin of cucumbers, but maybe they should. Refreshing and slightly sweet, cucumbers and melon make perfect milkshake partners in the Honeydew-Cucumber Shake with Cucumber Granita (page 131) and the Minted Cucumber–Lemon Shake (page 129). Even high summer's sweet corn makes an unexpected and delightful shake. Check out the Sweet Corn and Basil Shake (page 148).

A Word About the Recipes

Amid all this talk of milkshake modernization, let us not overlook the founding fathers (or would that be founding flavors?) of all milkshake-dom—vanilla, chocolate, and strawberry. No matter how inventive the shakes in this book may be, they owe a debt to the big three, which is why I have included recipes for them, along with my versions of classic coffee and peach shakes. After all, don't I owe the new generation of shakes a solid foundation and a sense of their own history?

Ice cream There are enough flavors in even the most modest super-market, and certainly at any ice cream shop, to make you dizzy conceiv-ing of new concoctions, but these recipes forgo esoteric or frivolous flavors like Quack Tracks and Dublin Mudslide. In fact, the majority of the shakes in this book rely on solid-citizen, available-absolutely-everywhere vanilla ice cream. No matter what the flavor, every scoop of ice cream and sorbet I used to develop the recipes came from the supermarket. Brands included Ben & Jerry's, Blue Bunny, Breyers, Dreyer's, Edy's, Häagen-Dazs, Hood, Tillamook, Trader Joe's, and Turkey Hill.

With that said, though, I am all for experimentation. That is part of what makes cooking, or in this case shaking, a joy. So if you encounter a particular flavor of ice cream, perhaps based on season, region, specialty product line, or limited run, and you think it would be good in a particular shake, by all means try it. For instance, in the autumn some brands sell pumpkin ice cream, which would be perfect for the Spiced Pumpkin Shake (page 150).

Milk Many milkshake purists insist on using whole milk. I don't. I tried whole milk, 2 percent, and 1 percent (no skim—you have to draw the line somewhere) in these recipes and neither my tasters nor I could detect a difference in texture or flavor. That is not surprising, given that the ratio of milk to ice cream and/or sorbet in my recipes is low, just ½ cup to 4 cups.

Texture You have probably seen milkshake recipes that call for a modest scoop or two of ice cream per shake, or for a great deal more liquid, perhaps a cup or more. Not mine. I prefer thick shakes, those that require a bit of suction when you first jab the straw into them. Shakes are not really made for gulping; it takes a little while to get one down, and by the time you approach the bottom of the glass, the consistency will be much looser than when you began. Of course, just because I like a thick shake doesn't mean you have to. If it suits your taste, use a little more liquid; as long as you don't go overboard (doubling the amount, or more), it will not affect the flavor negatively.

If you glance through the recipes, you'll notice the conspicuous absence of cookies, candy, or crunchies—any type of mix-in—added to the shakes. That is because I like my shakes smooth. Lumps, no matter how delectable, jar my delicate sensibilities. All is not lost if you insist on mix-ins, though—see The Cult of the Concrete (page 154). Concretes are all about the mix-ins.

It's worth noting that the consistencies of the shakes vary a little based on their ingredients. For instance, dried fruits such as the dates in the Date-Buttermilk Shake (page 140), or the prunes in the Prune-Armagnac Shake (page 133), or very dense fresh fruit such as the figs in the Fresh Fig Shake (page 107), or the avocado in the Avocado, Coconut, and Lime Shake (page 113) result in exceptionally thick, velvety consistencies. At the opposite end of the texture spectrum are shakes that include watery fruits, such as the honeydew melon in the Honeydew-Cucumber Shake with Cucumber Granita (page 131), or the cantaloupe in the Cantaloupe-Lemon Shake (page

134), or the tomato in the Tomato-Peach Shake (page 122). The consistencies of these shakes are looser than many of the others. And note that if the shake is made with all sorbet and no ice cream such as the Coconut Patty Shake (page 70), the texture will be a little bit rougher and less creamy, though in this case the cream of coconut compensates.

Frothiness In the course of developing the recipes and writing the book, I read a lot of definitions of milkshakes, many of which mentioned that the ingredients are beaten to a froth. Not here. Again, I let my strong preference for a thick texture lead the way, and the thicker the shake, the less likely that it will be really frothy.

If you are of the frothy persuasion, though, I can make two suggestions. First, some recipe writers suggest that adding ice to a shake makes it frothy. I tried it several times and noticed a little bit of extra froth, but the shakes were thinner (and colder). Second, try blending the shake at a high setting for an extra long time, say two minutes, to warm the mixture a bit (from the friction of the spinning blender blades) and incorporate more air, thereby increasing the froth factor. Again, though, your shake will end up with a relatively liquidy texture, and that is a sacrifice I'm not willing to make in the name of froth.

Measurements To standardize the recipes, I assume that one medium scoop of ice cream has a volume of $\frac{1}{4}$ pint ($\frac{1}{2}$ cup) and weighs 3 ounces/85 grams. It follows, then, that the full eight scoops in most recipes have a volume of 1 quart (4 cups) and weigh 24 ounces/680 grams. The weight of a $\frac{1}{2}$ cup volume scoop may vary based on the brand of ice cream and the amount of air incorporated into it, which is called overrun. (Ice cream has to have some air in it, otherwise it would be a solid, unpalatable mass.) Super-premium ice creams, such as Häagen-Dazs and Ben & Jerry's, trade on their rich, dense textures, which they achieve with relatively small overruns, so $\frac{1}{4}$ pint of such a brand will weigh slightly more than 3 ounces/85 grams, though not enough to damage the outcome of the recipe.

Another thing to keep in mind: the ounce measurements given for liquids and recipe yields are based on *liquid volume*, not weight. For other ingredients, such as ice cream, sorbet, honey, jam, sugar, fruit, nut butters, and the like, ounce measurements refer to *weight*. Metric measurements such as milliliters and grams are also provided.

Yields I bet you have noticed that all the recipe yields begin with the word "about." That is by design, because the yields vary based on a couple of factors. First is the brand of ice cream and its degree of overrun. Second is your scoops. If you don't measure them precisely, and really, who would for a milkshake? (not me, if I weren't writing recipes for them), then the chances are they will be a bit large or small, which will certainly affect the yield. The bulk of extra ingredients, such as fruit or Nutella, will cause some variation, as will the length of time that you blend the shake.

Give Your Shake a Fair Shake

I have lost count of the number of milkshakes I've blended recently, but it is certainly upward of two hundred. Along the way, I made some observations that should help you make a marvelous milkshake.

Ice If there are ice cubes in the recipe, as there are for the *batidos* and *licuados* in the "Shakes from Afar" chapter, put them in the blender and crush them before adding other ingredients. This way you will avoid big chunks in the drink.

Ingredient order In my experience, you will be better off adding liquids to the blender jar first. If there are viscous or solid flavorings in the recipe, such as honey or fruit, add them along with the liquid and blend them until they are very thoroughly incorporated before adding the ice cream and sorbet, which should always go into the jar last.

Pulsing and prodding I used a fleet of different blenders while developing the recipes, and the process was essentially the same in all of them. Once you have added the ice cream and sorbet, it's best to start blending by pulsing the motor to begin breaking them down. Unless your ice cream is really soft—too soft to achieve my preferred thick texture—you'll have to stop the blender, remove the lid, and use a utensil to mash the ice cream down into the jar—probably more than once. This will both pop any air pockets that formed and break the surface tension between the ice cream and the walls of the blender jar.

Once all the ingredients are incorporated, continue blending until you see that the mixture moves freely inside the jar. The longer you blend, the thinner the milkshake will become. Especially if there are no solid ingredients to integrate, I try to keep the blending time down to help ensure a thick consistency. This tenet doesn't necessarily apply to *batidos* and *licuados*, though. They generally contain so much fruit that the texture benefits from a longer blending time to thoroughly break down the solids.

Soften the ice cream The most important point in terms of process is to allow the ice cream and sorbet to soften slightly before making the shake. In my home freezer, which I have set to maintain a temperature of 0 degrees Fahrenheit (-18 degrees Celsius), the ice cream in a 1.5-quart (1.5-liter) container is right around 5 degrees Fahrenheit (-15 degrees Celsius). At that temperature, it is too firm to blend easily. After about twelve minutes at room temperature, the ice cream around the edges of the container looks melty and registers 12 to 14 degrees Fahrenheit (-11 to -10 degrees Celsius), on an instant-read thermometer. This is the ideal stage to balance ease of blending the ice cream with that prized thick consistency. I doubt that most people will be obsessive enough to measure the temperature of their ice cream, but everyone should be able to handle waiting a few moments until the edges appear a bit melty.

Keep Your Bananas at Bay—The Difference Between Smoothies and Shakes, According to Adam

Milkshakes and smoothies may look alike, and they may slurp alike, but in my mind, there is a very clear distinction between them. Ninety-five percent of the time, smoothies include fruit. In fact, it is the fruit that defines them. Other ingredients might be juice, ice, milk, or yogurt, and very often some banana, presumably added for the creamy texture it imparts to the mixture. There may also be some ice cream or frozen yogurt, but usually in small amounts. Because of the fruit, smoothies have an aura of health—vitamins, minerals, fiber, minimal sugar, and that sort of thing.

Ice cream, and now sorbet, defines a milkshake. If you're lucky, *lots* of ice cream. There is absolutely no pretense of healthfulness. A milkshake is an indulgence, plain and simple, and hallelujah for that! If there is fruit in a milkshake, and there may well be, it is usually in much smaller amounts than you'd find in a smoothie.

That is the difference, whittled down to a nub. Smoothies are about fruit; milkshakes are about ice cream.

I am equal opportunity in my love for cold, thick, well-flavored, slurpable drinks. And I do not even object to vitamins and minerals and fiber. So I like smoothies just fine. In fact, the *batido* and *licuado* recipes in the "Shakes from Afar" chapter are smoothies, for all intents and purposes.

But please, when it comes to the milkshakes, keep your bananas at bay.

The Soda Fountain Beverage Family Tree

Since we are distinguishing milkshakes from smoothies, how about a quick rundown of other ice cream parlor and soda fountain drinks, too? During the soda fountain heyday of the 1940s and 1950s, many soda jerks, as soda fountain workers were often called, developed their own variations on popular drinks, and they were fast and loose with the names. Because of the nomenclature variation from fountain to fountain and region to region, the lines between drink formulas—and names—are blurred. This is to say that the general definitions below are good indicators, but by no means set in stone. Some of these drinks, such as phosphates, are no longer common.

Cabinet The Rhode Island and southeastern Massachusetts name for a frappe. See Coffee- and Cabinet-Crazed Rhode Island, page 89, and Awful Awful Cabinets, page 98.

Concrete Dense frozen custard with myriad mix-ins such as candy, nuts, cookie pieces, and the like. In my experience, concretes are too thick to qualify as a beverage, though they are sometimes sold as such.

Egg cream A drink specific to the New York City area, made with milk, chocolate syrup, and carbonated water (seltzer, or soda water). Ironically, it contains neither egg nor cream. See Hal's Inauthentic Egg Cream, page 24.

Float Essentially the same thing as an ice cream soda, but often made with a flavored soft drink such as root beer, cola, orange soda, or grape soda, as opposed to carbonated water flavored with syrup.

Frappe The New England name for the same mixture of ice cream, milk, and flavoring that is called a milkshake in most of the United States. See New England Nomenclature, page 85.

Freeze Essentially the same thing as a slush, but with the addition of a dairy ingredient such as milk, cream, sherbet, ice cream, or frozen yogurt.

Frosted A term that arose in the 1930s as the practice of adding ice cream to (previously ice creamless) milkshakes became more and more popular. With ice cream added, the milkshake became a "frosted," which essentially became an alternate name for a milkshake, used during the 1940s and 1950s in some regions.

Ice cream soda A mixture of carbonated water, syrup, and ice cream. The ice cream interacts with the carbonation to create a frothy head.

Malted A milkshake with malt powder added.

Milkshake The Mack Daddy of soda fountain drinks, in my humble opinion. A blended or whipped mixture of ice cream, milk, and flavorings (often syrup).

Phosphate A carbonated drink made by the soda jerk from carbonated water and a flavoring syrup, with or without some phosphoric acid for extra tartness. Chocolate, vanilla, lime, lemon, and cherry were particularly popular flavors.

Slush A mixture of water, juice or syrup flavoring, and crushed ice. Fruit flavors and garish colors are common, and sometimes carbonated water replaces the still water. Slushes are often sold at convenience stores and gas stations.

Hal's Inauthentic Egg Cream

My father was old school. Raised in the 1920s and 1930s on the Grand Concourse in the Bronx, his automatic reply to any question I asked about his childhood was "I don't remember." So imagine my shock the day I asked him about that old New York classic fountain drink, the egg cream, made of chocolate syrup, milk, and seltzer. My father, Hal "I Don't Remember" Ried, gushed. He swooned. He remembered!

Without a moment's hesitation Dad recalled stopping at a Bronx soda fountain for egg creams on the way home from school. He laughed over the fact that egg creams contained neither eggs nor cream, and he said that it was imperative to drink them fast, before the frothy head went flat.

Then Dad made a surprise move. "Here, I'll show you," he said, and started pulling containers from the fridge. Now, it's worth a pause here to note that any true egg cream aficionado would insist that Fox's U-Bet chocolate syrup is the only acceptable brand for the job. Dad knew that, but this was Connecticut in the 1970s, not the Grand Concourse in the 1930s; Hershey's syrup was what we had, so Hershey's is what we used. And that wasn't the only affront to authenticity, because rather than using seltzer from a proper soda siphon, Dad made our egg creams with the bubbly water on hand—Perrier. How Connecticut is that?

Anyway, in tall glasses Dad made dense, dark chocolate milk, using about ¾ cup (6 ounces/180 milliliters) milk and ¼ cup (2 ounces/60 milliliters) syrup for each of us. Then he filled each glass almost all the way with bubbly water (there was a bit more bubbly than there was chocolate milk), leaving just enough space at the top for the frothy, fragile head. And then we gulped them down in unison.

· · · · · · · · ·
MAKES 2
· · · · · · · · ·

With all due respect to Fox's U-Bet, I advise you to use whatever chocolate syrup you have on hand. Better an ersatz egg cream than no egg cream at all.

1 ½ cups cold whole or lowfat milk
(about 12 ounces/360 milliliters)

½ cup chocolate syrup
(about 4 ounces/120 milliliters)

3 cups seltzer water, or more
(about 24 ounces/ 750 milliliters)

In each of two tall glasses, mix ¾ cup (6 ounces/180 milliliters) milk with ¼ cup (2 ounces/60 milliliters) syrup to blend well. With a long spoon stir the chocolate milk in one glass to create a vortex, and quickly add 1 ½ cups (12 ounces/375 milliliters) seltzer, or as much as necessary to nearly fill the glass, leaving just enough space at the top for the head. Quickly repeat the process with the chocolate milk in the second glass, and serve at once.

EQUIPMENT

AND A KEY

INGREDIENT

OR TWO

As the editor in charge of kitchen equipment testing at *Cook's Illustrated* magazine for ten years, and in my ongoing role as the kitchen equipment specialist on the PBS shows *America's Test Kitchen* and *Cook's Country from America's Test Kitchen*, I have logged some serious hours testing and evaluating just about every small kitchen appliance, piece of cookware, and utensil you can think of. With that kind of background, there is no way I could stay mum about the hardware you'll need to make a great milkshake, so here are a few observations.

Blenders

I researched and tested blenders at *Cook's Illustrated* and *America's Test Kitchen*, and developing the recipes in this book was a terrific refresher course. I used eight different blenders from five manufacturers, as well as three drink mixers like the ones you see cranking out the shakes at ice cream parlors. While I would be hard-pressed to name the blender of your dreams without first performing a full battery of comprehensive tests on a wide range of models, I can certainly offer a laundry list of desirable design features to keep in mind the next time you go blender shopping.

First, the jar, which some people call the carafe. The shape of the jar is important to the blender's performance. I strongly prefer tall jars that are wide at the top and have angled sides that taper to a narrow bottom. A small base means that the food can't go far; it increases contact between the contents of the blender and the spinning blades, which increases efficiency. By comparison, the excess space at the base of a wide blender jar (or the workbowl of a food processor) allows the ingredients to spread more laterally, which is a little less efficient. A narrow base also helps force the ingredients upward in the jar, allowing the spinning blades to create a vortex that helps incorporate air for smoother texture.

Ideally, the interior surface of the jar walls will have some type of built-in undulation or irregularity, as opposed to being completely smooth. This might take the form of small protrusions called flutes, inward-facing indentations molded right into the glass, or the shape of the jar itself might be uneven. The purpose of the irregularity is to interrupt the vortex inside the jar, thereby forcing the contents downward onto the blades. Again, it's all about increased contact between the food and the blades.

In terms of materials, go for glass if you have the option. It's heavier than plastic, which is the other popular material for blender jars, and therefore more stable in the blender base. Glass also resists scratching better than plastic. Last, glass is transparent, so you can see inside while you're blending, which is helpful. I dislike the stainless steel jars that come with some blender models because they are opaque.

In my mind, the larger the capacity of the jar, the better. Shoot for a 40-ounce minimum. Also, I prefer jars with removable bases and blade assemblies for their ease of cleaning. As an aside, regardless of whether the base is sealed or removable, a great way to clean a blender jar is to fill it about halfway with warm water, add a couple of drops of liquid dish detergent, and let 'er rip at high speed for about twenty seconds. Most of the food residue will pour right out with the soapy water. Give the jar a rinse or a light cleaning, and you're good to go.

No matter how large the blender jar, or what shape it is, don't fill it up more than about two-thirds to the top (many experts suggest no more than halfway to the top) because you have to leave space for the contents to move upward. This is especially critical if you are blending something hot.

That brings us to the lid. I suggest holding the lid in place whenever the blender is running (and using a kitchen towel or pot holder to do so whenever the contents of the blender are hot). Better to stand by the blender for half a minute while you blend than spend an hour cleaning milkshake off the ceilings, walls, windows, cabinets, counters, and floors. Trust me—I speak from experience. And I was making chicken liver mousse, not milkshakes. The tiny kitchen was covered with pureed liver. It was *not* pretty.

One more thing—the blades. Blender blades are generally set at several angles, so they cut on multiple planes at once (as opposed to food processor blades, which are usually set at a single angle). In my testing I have never identified a particular blade design as being responsible for more or less effective blending, but as a minor point, I can imagine that the more angles, the better.

Now on to the blender base, which houses the motor and controls. I wouldn't worry too much about the power rating of the motor, usually expressed in watts. Manufacturers often make a big deal out of the wattage, but as I understand it, watts really measure the amount of power the motor draws from the outlet, not the amount of power it generates. The efficiency with which the motor operates—how it transforms the power it draws into output—depends largely on the motor's design. Really, I think the design of the jar is more important to performance than the wattage.

Nor have I found any direct correlation between wattage and noise. My theory is that the noise level generated by a particular blender has more to do with its insulation than its power rating. My best advice here is to listen to a demo model at the store before plunking down the plastic to determine whether you can live with the decibels.

Blender controls come in four basic styles, of which small buttons may be the most familiar. They are also the only option I really dislike. The buttons work fine, but they make the face of the blender base a bear to clean. The second option, flush touchpad controls, are particularly easy to use and clean. I have heard, however, that they can get a bit wonky over time, so I can't vouch for them over the long haul. Toggle switches and twist knobs are the third and fourth and, I think, best options. They are simple and easy to use, and they seem to split the difference between ease of cleaning and durability.

Some blenders offer a huge number of speeds. The ancient, harvest-gold clunker that I've used for more than twenty-five years, for instance, has fourteen speeds. Of those, I think I have only ever used two—low, and high. I have also used the pulse feature, which is nice, but a luxury, since it's easy to mimic by turning the blender on and off. If all those speeds float your boat, there is nothing wrong with having them, but I don't think they do much to enhance the blender's performance.

So there you have it. If you need to buy a blender, I suggest choosing one with a large-capacity, tapered glass jar with a removable base and blade assembly, and toggle switch or twist-knob controls. A pulse feature is nice if you can get it, and I wouldn't spend extra money to get extra speeds beyond low and high.

Finally, a banal reminder: you are going to be using a blender, whose very sharp blades, spinning at very high speeds, can cause very bad damage to very tender human fingers. And to most kitchen utensils you stick down into the blender jar while it's running, too. And if you were, heaven forfend, to stick a metal utensil into the jar, you would be *really* sorry because you could potentially create a real safety—and cleanliness—disaster. So whenever you need to open a blender to check or stir its contents, make absolutely certain that the blade has stopped spinning before putting anything into the jar. While you're at it, take care when cleaning a blender jar, too. It's got *blades*, people. Sharp, pointy blades.

Magic Bullet

Every night owl, myself included, knows that the late, late night TV landscape is the almost-exclusive province of long, droning infomercials advertising miracle skin creams, ab crunchers, lawn trimmers, foreclosed property auctions, and multipurpose kitchen gadgets that promise to "peel, chop, slice, dice, julienne, blend, whip, grind, and more!"

Cool, rational equipment tester that I am, I tend to gravitate toward more established kitchen products and pass right by this type of thing. That is, until I got my hands on the Magic Bullet, the high-torque mini blender with multiple blades and attachments galore, from "party mugs" to vegetable juicers—twenty-one pieces in all. I thought it would be a kick to try out some milkshakes and *batidos* in the Magic Bullet, and the darned thing really surprised me.

Here's how you set it up. There are several different-sized cups, plus four "party mugs," which you can use to both prepare and serve smoothies and frozen drinks. Place the ingredients in the cup, screw on the blade assembly, invert it onto the small power base, and press it down onto the base to operate. I have to be honest: the Bullet makes an impressive shake. You have to pick up the whole thing and shake it as it blends to make sure all the ingredients incorporate, but it is small and light, so that's easy, and it was much less messy than opening a blender jar and poking at the contents with a flexible spatula or spoon. All the shakes I made were very thick and smooth, and there was something to this business of making the shake and drinking it from the same vessel. It really did minimize cleanup. The regular blending cups were too small to accommodate the full quantity of a recipe from the book, but they handled half quantities just fine, and there was a larger blender jar for larger quantities.

Fruit *batidos* made with ice cubes were less successful. Even after a lot of blending and shaking, there were still large chunks of ice left, though the rest of the mixture was blended and smooth. In defense of the Bullet, though, I will say that the ice cubes from my trays are large, about $1\frac{1}{2}$ inches by $1\frac{1}{4}$ inches (4 centimeters by 3.25 centimeters), and there is a bit of small print in the Bullet instruction manual recommending the use of small ice cubes for the best results.

Would I replace my regular blender with the Magic Bullet? Probably not, because I'd miss the large capacity of the jar. If I planned to make single-serving shakes frequently, though, the Bullet would be pretty tempting, especially if my ice cubes were smaller! See www.buythebullet.com.

Drink Mixers

Drink mixers are usually seen on duty at ice cream parlors or soda fountains. It's that tall gizmo, with a stainless steel cup that hooks to the front, a top-mounted motor, and a spindle with one or more agitators that reaches down into the cup. This appliance's main goal in life is to make cold, thick drinks like shakes and smoothies, though manufacturers often trumpet other, and in my opinion, unlikely uses such as mixing eggs or pancake batter.

After experimenting with three mixers, I reached the conclusion that they don't offer enough of an advantage over a blender to justify buying and storing one. First, the cups are small, with maximum capacities of $1\frac{3}{4}$ cups (425 milliliters) or less, so they are essentially able to handle just one shake at a time. Since the recipes in this book yield upward of three cups to serve several people, the mixers would not accommodate the full quantity of a recipe. In fact, I was just barely able to squeeze in a half quantity without spilling milkshake all over the counter. Second, I found them messier to use than a blender—whenever I removed the cup, the spindle dripped on the counter (although I quickly learned to have a sponge at hand and swoop in with it immediately, but that was a nuisance). Third, neither my tasters nor I detected any textural superiority over shakes from a blender, though I did think the shakes were a little colder than their blended brethren. Last, I am disinclined to purchase single-purpose appliances, unless it's something like a waffle maker, without which you simply cannot make that item. Heck, I even slice mushrooms and strawberries with my egg slicer, which triples its usefulness (actually, I will never slice mushrooms with a knife again; the egg slicer is the way to go, but that is another story for another book).

If I were a milkshake addict with money to burn, and I absolutely *had* to have a drink mixer, then I'd buy a double spindle model, so at least I could make two flavors at once, or serve more than one person at a time. But believe me, if and when I hit the jackpot, that double spindle drink mixer would only come after I spent some quality time and a bundle of cash at my local Aston Martin dealership.

Ice Cream Scoops

A milkshake regimen will certainly put your ice cream scoop to work. Notice that I said "to work," not "to the test." That's because we are softening the ice cream a little before making shakes with it, and even a soup spoon can serve up softened ice cream. Fresh from the freezer, hard-as-a-rock ice cream is the real test of an ice cream scoop, or "dipper," in the parlance of the professional ice cream world. Still, why not buy the best one you can?

There are three primary scoop styles: basic; those with a spring-loaded release mechanism; and the spade. Of course designs within each type vary as well. Basic scoops are as simple as it gets—a bowl attached to a handle, with no moving parts. The bowl should have a thin leading edge to dig into hard ice cream easily, a shape that creates neat balls of ice cream, and the ability to release the ice cream easily (so that it doesn't break a brittle sugar cone, if that happens to be the serving vessel). In this format, the shape of the bowl varies from model to model.

Spring-loaded release dippers add a blade that moves along the interior surface of the bowl when it's activated by a lever in the handle, allowing the bowl to eject its contents. The bowls on this type of scoop are generally semi-spherical. If you opt for this type, find a model that feels solid, with all the parts firmly attached, a comfortable handle with a lever that is easy to squeeze, and a smooth, sweeping blade action. It's worth noting that the bowls (in both this type and the basic design) come in various sizes. Smaller spring-loaded release dippers are terrific for equally portioning stiff doughs and batters, say for cookies or muffins, and even scoopable foods such as tuna salad or mac and cheese.

The last style, spades, have relatively flat, open bowls that allow them to scoop large quantities at once. These are great for serving gelato or softened ice cream in large containers, or for incorporating mix-ins. For use at home, though, they present a major disadvantage in that most of the models I've tried are too big to fit into a pint container.

When it comes to scoops, I think basic is best, and my favorite models are made by Zeroll. Both their Original Ice Cream Scoop and their nonstick-coated Zerolon scoops are terrific, and widely available at stores with a good selection of cookware and online at www.zeroll.com. The handles are strong and comfortable, so they provide excellent leverage for digging into hard ice cream (and they work equally well for both righties and lefties). The bowls have a slight beak at the front, with a thin edge, and they dig in easily and form neat balls of ice cream. Easy release of the ice cream is reliable because the scoops are filled with a defrosting fluid that conducts the heat from your hand—or, if your ice cream is rock solid, the heat from a short soak in warm tap water, which speeds things along. The only disadvantage of the Zeroll scoops, and it's minor, is that they are not dishwasher safe.

Freezer Temperature and Thermometers

If you are going to be making many milkshakes, as indeed I hope this book moves you to do, it's worth devoting a bit of thought to your freezer. This is especially so if you constantly open and shut the door, as this causes temperature fluctuations that challenge any freezer. Here, then, are a couple of pointers on maximizing your freezer's performance.

For both efficiency and optimum food safety, experts agree that the freezer temperature should be set to 0 degrees Fahrenheit (-18 degrees Celsius), or even a couple of degrees below that. You can give your freezer a leg up on temperature maintenance if you keep it reasonably full. Not *packed* full, mind you, but about two-thirds full. The mass of frozen goods holds the cold to help keep the overall temperature stable. At the same time, though, make sure to leave a little space around all the items in the freezer to allow the cold air to circulate easily. Also in the name of air flow, do not push anything right up against the vent in the back of the freezer because that impedes the entry and circulation of cold air.

Every freezer has areas that are cooler and warmer. Based on tests conducted for *America's Test Kitchen*, the coldest spot is the center rear. If you can bear the inconvenience of having to reach way back there all the time, this would be a great spot to keep larger containers of ice cream, say 1.5 quarts (1.5 liters) or more. Conversely, the shelves on the door are the warmest zone, so this is where I keep items that I use frequently, like butter and bread. It's also where I keep pint containers of sorbet and ice cream, so long as I know that I want them to be on the soft side for milkshakes, and that I'll use them up fairly quickly.

Monitoring the temperature scenario with a freezer thermometer is a great idea. The thermometers are generally pretty cheap—many cost just five or six dollars. In addition to being accurate, a good thermometer has a clear display (digital models, which are more expensive at around twenty dollars, have the advantage over dial-face thermometers here) and some means by which to secure it in the freezer. In my freezer, shelf space is way too precious to sacrifice to a thermometer that sits on or hangs from a shelf, not to mention the fact that knocking it over every time I grab a nearby item drives me insane. That's why my vote for best thermometer goes to the Oxo Good Grips Refrigerator/Freezer Thermometer. At thirteen dollars it is mid-priced, but it's so well designed that it's worth the extra money. It affixes to the inside wall of the freezer (or refrigerator, if you'd prefer to use it there) with a suction cup that actually keeps it attached. The graphics on the face are clear, easy to read, and even illuminated by the freezer light because the back panel is made of frosted glass that allows the light through. Best of all, the thermometer is mounted on a hinge that allows it to pivot forward or all the way back against the wall when you are loading or unloading the freezer. The thermometer is widely available in cookware stores, and online at www.oxo.com.

Ingredients

As you undertake your milkshake odyssey, you'll use a lot of vanilla ice cream—the foundation for many of the recipes in the book, as well as vanilla extract and spices. Here are my thoughts on those items.

Vanilla ice cream Leafing through the recipes you may notice that I call for different types of vanilla ice cream for different shakes. If you can easily accommodate this instruction, then do, because I chose the type of vanilla that goes best with the flavors in the shake. With that said, though, let's not make mountains out of mole hills. If you're in the mood for a shake, and you happen to have a different type of vanilla ice cream in the freezer than what I call for, by all means, use what you have and blend on! It might not be the absolute pinnacle of pairings, but c'mon—it's a milkshake, and it's going to taste good no matter what type of vanilla you use. It's good to have the information, but not to be a prisoner to it.

Okay, that's our reality check. Now on to the various vanillas. On the ice cream containers you're likely to see the words "French," "custard," "original," "vanilla bean," "homemade," "natural," "golden," and "double." Unfortunately, nomenclature is something of a moving target because it's not consistent from brand to brand—one brand's "natural" could be another brand's "original." That makes it almost impossible to assign each word an ironclad definition. Yet there does exist a major divide between "French" or "custard" style and all the others that is consistent and useful to know.

French or custard vanilla has a relatively high proportion of egg yolks and butterfat (12.5 percent to 17 percent for the latter). Its texture is dense and especially creamy, and its color has a yellow hue from the yolks. The other types will generally have a smaller proportion of yolks, or none at all, and a little less butterfat (11.6 percent to 12.3 percent). Consequently, the ice cream will have a lighter flavor, texture, and color. Compared to French vanilla, it may seem lean on the tongue (although added gums and stabilizers can, and often do, make up for that). Vanilla bean ice cream has added visual appeal from tiny flecks of vanilla bean, though in my experience I'd be hard put to notice any boost in vanilla flavor from them.

In my mind, if a shake has relatively delicate flavors, say white peach or honeydew melon, they'd probably be overwhelmed (or at least challenged) by the richness of French vanilla. In those cases, I opt for lighter original or vanilla bean. On the other hand, shakes with more assertive flavors, say prune-armagnac, or spiced pumpkin, benefit from the yolky French-style vanilla, which is better able to stand up to the other ingredients.

Vanilla extract To me, a judicious amount of vanilla extract benefits sweet foods just as profoundly as salt enhances savory dishes. If you are careful not to use so much that the vanilla becomes its own distinct flavor element (unless that's your goal, of course), it brings a subtle but essential depth, roundness, and balance to sweets. Like salt, it brings up the overall flavor of the dish by making the major players taste more like themselves. For instance, without vanilla the sour cherries in the Sour Cherry and Sour Cream Shake (page 144) fall a little flat, and the Marsala in the Zabaglione Shake (page 152) seems a bit dim. And in some shakes, like the Ballistic Vanilla (page 40), it is a flavor that is out loud and proud!

From researching vanilla extract for a tasting story in *Cook's Illustrated*, I know that the overall flavor of vanilla results from more than four hundred chemical compounds. The most dominant among them—the one that would make you say "Oh yeah, that's vanilla," is called vanillin. Vanilla beans, which are the seed pods of a climbing vine related to the orchid, are the natural source of vanillin, but it is also possible to cheaply manufacture it.

Generally speaking, pure vanilla extracts rely on natural, and expensive, vanilla beans for flavor, while cheaper imitation vanilla is based on synthetic vanillin. The great curiosity of the tasting was the strong showing of imitation vanilla among the tasting panel. Because synthetic vanillin is cheaper than the real stuff, manufacturers can afford to use more of it in imitation vanilla, which translated to some tasters as a stronger vanilla flavor.

Despite the punch of the fake stuff, most experts favor pure vanilla extract, and so do I. To my palate it has more nuance, fragrance, and character than imitation, which strikes me as one-dimensional and unrefined in comparison. I don't have a strong allegiance to any particular brand (though I like the pure vanilla from Penzeys Spices a lot, and usually use it if I have the option—see www.penzeys.com), but for all of these recipes, especially those where vanilla is a real flavor player, I suggest using pure vanilla extract.

Spices On the topic of spices, I have one word for you. F-R-E-S-H. You've read this a thousand times, and now you can make it a thousand and one. It's that important. Old spices lack chutzpah. No spunk. Pas de get-up-and-go. Spices derive their flavor and character from essential oils that begin to dissipate as soon as the whole spice is ground to a powder, so for the best flavor, you should replace your ground spices often.

Many serious cooks insist on using only whole spices, which they toast and then grind as needed. This is indeed a great way to optimize the spices' flavor, but anybody who declares the process a nuisance gets no argument from me. That's why I use, for the most part, ground spices. But I try to both buy them right, and then treat them right at home. Here are my suggestions on those fronts.

First, if you have the option, try to buy spices in quantities that you will use up within six months (some cooks will tell you three months), and certainly, if a spice has been around for a year or more, replace it. If there is a spice shop within reach (I'm lucky enough to have two within easy biking distance), that's the best possible place to buy, since the products are likely to be fresher. Second best would be an ethnic market—in my area, Indian and Middle Eastern markets often sell spices—or a store that sells spices in bulk, since the turnover is likely to be high. As far as I'm concerned, the familiar bottles of ground spices in the supermarket are the last choice, because who knows how long they have been hanging around. I understand, though, that this is probably the only option for many people, in which case I suggest buying small containers that you'll use up quickly.

Air, light, heat, and moisture are natural enemies to spices, especially to ground spices, because they accelerate flavor deterioration. That's why open racks are actually a poor storage system for spices, particularly when the rack is stationed near the stove—a natural source of heat and moisture. It's better to keep spices in airtight containers in cool, dark, dry cupboards or drawers. If a drawer is home to your spices, consider writing the name and purchase date of each spice on sticky dots and affixing the dots to the tops of the jar lids. This will save you the frustration of having to lift each jar to read the label when you search for specific spices.

BASIC SHAKES

Ballistic Vanilla Shake

More than just basic vanilla, this shake is ballistic vanilla. Vanilla extract and eggy "French" vanilla ice cream (sometimes called "custard" style) provide unmistakable depth of flavor that gives vanilla lovers, or any ice cream lover, reason to rejoice.

½ cup cold whole or lowfat milk (about 4 ounces/ 125 milliliters)

2 teaspoons pure vanilla extract

8 medium scoops French vanilla ice cream (about 1 quart/ 24 ounces/680 grams), softened until just melty at the edges

MAKES ABOUT 3½ CUPS | 28 OUNCES | 850 MILLILITERS

Place the milk, vanilla extract, and ice cream in a blender and pulse several times to begin breaking up the ice cream. With the blender motor off, use a flexible spatula to mash the mixture down onto the blender blades. Continue pulsing, stopping, and mashing until the mixture is well blended, thick, and moves easily in the blender jar, roughly 30 to 90 seconds. Pour into a chilled glass or glasses, and serve at once.

Extra Rich Variation

Follow the recipe for the Ballistic Vanilla Shake, substituting cold half-and-half or heavy cream for the milk.

Malted Variation

Follow the recipe for the Ballistic Vanilla Shake, adding 2 tablespoons (about 1 ounce/28 grams) of malted milk powder to the blender with the milk and vanilla extract and blending for a moment before adding the vanilla ice cream and continuing to blend.

Facing page: from left to right, Stupendous Strawberry, Classic Chocolate, and Ballistic Vanilla shakes.

Classic Chocolate Shake

I can burn through hours . . . days . . . weeks! . . . reading about food on Web sites and blogs. One day I was cruising around chowhound.com and came upon a thread hotly debating the "correct" formula for a chocolate shake. Vanilla ice cream, milk, and chocolate syrup? Chocolate ice cream, milk, and chocolate syrup? Chocolate ice cream and milk, hold the syrup? I even saw assertions that the formula varied regionally—vanilla ice cream with syrup in the midwest and south, and chocolate ice cream with syrup in the north, with Maryland as the north/south dividing line.

I doubt there is a definitive answer to this issue, but I couldn't agree more that different shakes, all called "chocolate," can have very different flavors. So I decided to go with the flow and include two basic chocolate shake recipes in the book. This version, with a small portion of chocolate sorbet in place of the syrup (there is my two cents) and vanilla ice cream, has the lighter chocolate flavor of the two.

½ cup cold whole or lowfat milk (about 4 ounces/ 125 milliliters)

¼ teaspoon pure vanilla extract

7 medium scoops original vanilla or vanilla bean ice cream (about 1 ¾ pints/ 21 ounces/595 grams), softened until just melty at the edges

1 medium scoop chocolate sorbet (about ¼ pint/ 3 ounces/85 grams), softened until just melty at the edges

Place the milk, vanilla extract, ice cream, and sorbet in a blender and pulse several times to begin breaking up the ice cream and sorbet. With the blender motor off, use a flexible spatula to mash the mixture down onto the blender blades. Continue pulsing, stopping, and mashing until the mixture is well blended, thick, and moves easily in the blender jar, roughly 30 to 90 seconds. Pour into a chilled glass or glasses, and serve at once.

Extra Rich Variation

Follow the recipe for the Classic Chocolate Shake, substituting cold half-and-half or heavy cream for the milk.

Malted Variation

Follow the recipe for the Classic Chocolate Shake, adding 2 tablespoons (about 1 ounce/28 grams) of malted milk powder to the blender with the milk and vanilla extract and blending for a moment before adding the ice cream and sorbet and continuing to blend.

Serious Chocolate Shake

Although the Classic Chocolate Shake (page 42) is a great chocolate shake, this is a great !!!***#####!!! C-H-O-C-O-L-A-T-E !!!***#####!!! shake. There is nothing timid about the flavor here—it is chocolate down to its very last corpuscle, just the way I like it.

1/2 cup cold whole or lowfat milk (about 4 ounces/125 milliliters)

1/4 teaspoon pure vanilla extract

4 medium scoops chocolate ice cream (about 1 pint/ 12 ounces/340 grams), softened until just melty at the edges

4 medium scoops chocolate sorbet (about 1 pint/ 12 ounces/340 grams), softened until just melty at the edges

MAKES ABOUT 3 1/2 CUPS | 28 OUNCES | 850 MILLILITERS

Place the milk, vanilla extract, ice cream, and sorbet in a blender and pulse several times to begin breaking up the ice cream and sorbet. With the blender motor off, use a flexible spatula to mash the mixture down onto the blender blades. Continue pulsing, stopping, and mashing until the mixture is well blended, thick, and moves easily in the blender jar, roughly 30 to 90 seconds. Pour into a chilled glass or glasses, and serve at once.

Extra Rich Variation

Follow the recipe for the *Serious* Chocolate Shake, substituting cold half-and-half or heavy cream for the milk.

Malted Variation

Follow the recipe for the *Serious* Chocolate Shake, adding 2 tablespoons (about 1 ounce/28 grams) of malted milk powder to the blender with the milk and vanilla extract and blending for a moment before adding the ice cream and sorbet and continuing to blend.

Stupendous Strawberry Shake

Deep red, broad-shouldered, and shapely though they are, the flavor of supermarket strawberries often falls short of the promise in their appearance.

Save for the brief period every year when local strawberries are in season and ripe, I think strawberry sorbet tastes more like the real thing . . . than the real thing. With a triple hit of strawberry from the ice cream, sorbet, and jam, you get much stronger berry flavor in this shake than the berries themselves could possibly muster. Strawberries are not terribly acidic, so a small hit of lemon juice enhances their flavor even more.

½ cup cold whole or lowfat milk (about 4 ounces/125 milliliters)

2 tablespoons strawberry jam or preserves (about 1 ounce/28 grams)

1 teaspoon freshly squeezed lemon juice

4 medium scoops strawberry ice cream (about 1 pint/ 12 ounces/340 grams), softened until just melty at the edges

4 medium scoops strawberry sorbet (about 1 pint/ 12 ounces/340 grams), softened until just melty at the edges

MAKES ABOUT 3½ CUPS | 28 OUNCES | 850 MILLILITERS

Place the milk, jam, and lemon juice in a blender and blend to mix thoroughly, about 15 seconds. Add the ice cream and sorbet and pulse several times to begin breaking them up. With the blender motor off, use a flexible spatula to mash the mixture down onto the blender blades. Continue pulsing, stopping, and mashing until the mixture is well blended, thick, and moves easily in the blender jar, roughly 30 to 90 seconds. Pour into a chilled glass or glasses, and serve at once.

A Shot in the Dark by Every Other Name

For as long as I can remember, I have always called a shot of espresso in a cup of coffee a Shot in the Dark. When I was developing the recipe for the Shot in the Dark Coffee Shake (see facing page), though, I was reminded that many of the cool coffee houses in the Northwest have their own names for their coffee concoctions.

When I started investigating nomenclature online and on the street, I learned that my Shot in the Dark goes by a host of aliases. Depending on where you are, you may see a shot of espresso in a cup of coffee called a Red Eye, a Black Eye, a Boilermaker, a Boilerhouse, a Speed Ball, an All-Nighter, a Black Fandango, a Bull Dog, a Single By-Pass (in which case a double shot is a Double By-Pass, and a triple shot is a Triple By-Pass), a Canadiano, a Coffee Suicide, a Cup o' Crack, a Dead Man Walking, a Depth Charge, an Eclectic Witch Water, an Early Shirley, an Eye Opener, a Hammerhead, a Kick-in-the-Asspresso, a Lazarus, a Mad Max, a Morning Face Maker, an Overdrive, a Train Wreck, a Java Jolt, a Kick Start, a City Buzz, a Coal Burner, a Slingblade, or an Autobahn.

Shot in the Dark Coffee Shake

Most of my family lives in hardcore coffee country, the Pacific Northwest. At coffee houses on nearly every corner in every town, it's common to see caffeine-craving customers order a Shot in the Dark, which is a shot of espresso in a cup of regular coffee. Blend in some coffee ice cream and it sounds like the makings of a great basic coffee shake to me!

By the way, you also see people loading up their coffee with two or three shots of espresso. Depending on who you ask, a double shot in coffee is called Black Eye or a Red Eye, a triple shot is either a Glass Eye or a Dead Eye, and a quadruple shot earns the moniker Heart Stopper.

In barista-speak, making an espresso is called "pulling" an espresso.

¼ cup double-strength brewed coffee, at room temperature (about 2 ounces/60 milliliters)

2 shots freshly pulled espresso, at room temperature (4 tablespoons/ 2 ounces/60 milliliters)

8 medium scoops coffee ice cream (about 1 quart/24 ounces/ 680 grams), softened until just melty at the edges

MAKES ABOUT 3½ CUPS | 28 OUNCES | 850 MILLILITERS

Place the coffee, espresso, and ice cream in a blender and pulse several times to begin breaking up the ice cream. With the blender motor off, use a flexible spatula to mash the mixture down onto the blender blades. Continue pulsing, stopping, and mashing until the mixture is well blended, thick, and moves easily in the blender jar, roughly 30 to 90 seconds. Pour into a chilled glass or glasses, and serve at once.

How About a Horlicks?

Malted milk powder is a straightforward blend of barley, wheat flour, and milk, mixed into a mash and evaporated until it's a dry powder. The flavor is distinctive yet mellow, round, rich, and slightly sweet, and it mixes well with other flavors such as chocolate, vanilla, or coffee.

Historically, malted milk is rooted in a single English company called Horlicks, founded in the United States in 1873 by brothers James and William Horlick, and still in operation today. In 1883 the Horlicks received a U.S. patent for their product, and in 1887 they trademarked the name "malted milk," quite an improvement over the original name, Diastoid. Later malted milk became known as an easily digested, nutritious health drink for infants and the elderly, and eventually as a popular additive to another healthy drink of the period, the milkshake.

In 1890 James Horlick returned to England to arrange for the importation of U.S.-made malted milk, and by 1908 had established a factory to manufacture it there. Over the next few years, Horlicks malted milk was provisioned in several high-profile expeditions to the North and South Poles, as well as during World War I, as a nutritional drink for both troops on the front and citizens at home. By 1945 both James and William Horlick had died, and the U.S. branch of their business had been absorbed by the British branch.

In 1969 Horlicks was acquired by the Beecham Group, which, through a series of subsequent mergers, ended up as GlaxoSmithKline, the current owner of the brand. The product is so firmly rooted in English culture that both the powder and the drink made with it are called Horlicks, much as Americans often call tissues "Kleenex" and photocopies "Xeroxes."

Triple Peach Shake

This shake benefits from a peachy triple play—the sorbet buoys the ice cream, and just a touch of peach jam hits the flavor right into the territory of perfectly ripe, juicy, perfumed peaches purchased in August at a roadside farmstand in Georgia.

½ cup cold whole or lowfat milk (about 4 ounces/125 milliliters)

1½ tablespoons peach jam or preserves (about ¾ ounce/20 grams)

¼ teaspoon pure vanilla extract

2 medium scoops peach ice cream (about ½ pint/6 ounces/170 grams), softened until just melty at the edges

6 medium scoops peach sorbet (about 1½ pints/18 ounces/510 grams), softened until just melty at the edges

MAKES ABOUT 3½ CUPS | 28 OUNCES | 850 MILLILITERS

Place the milk, jam, and vanilla extract in a blender and blend to mix thoroughly, about 15 seconds. Add the ice cream and sorbet and pulse several times to begin breaking them up. With the blender motor off, use a flexible spatula to mash the mixture down onto the blender blades. Continue pulsing, stopping, and mashing until the mixture is well blended, thick, and moves easily in the blender jar, roughly 30 to 90 seconds. Pour into a chilled glass or glasses, and serve at once.

Triple Peach–Buttermilk Variation

Buttermilk adds a gentle tang that plays beautifully against the sweet peach flavor.

Follow the recipe for the Triple Peach Shake, substituting cold whole or lowfat buttermilk for the milk, increasing the peach ice cream to 6 scoops (about 1½ pints/18 ounces/510 grams), and decreasing the sorbet to 2 scoops (about ½ pint/6 ounces/170 grams).

VANILLA SHAKES

Lavender Honey–Vanilla Shake

Not surprisingly, the flavor of culinary lavender is herbaceous and floral, so it underscores beautifully the floral notes in the honey. I am lucky enough to have lavender growing in the yard by my house, so I don't have to go farther than the front step to pick some. If you're less fortunate in the lavender department, it's available online at www.atouchofprovence.com. Actually, at the same Web site you can even purchase a jar of lavender honey, and forgo the whole first step in the recipe.

½ cup honey (about 6 ounces/170 grams)

3 tablespoons fresh or dried lavender flowers (reserve a few small leaves for garnish, if desired; about ¼ ounce/7 grams)

½ cup cold whole or lowfat milk (about 4 ounces/125 milliliters)

¼ teaspoon pure vanilla extract

½ teaspoon freshly squeezed lemon juice

8 medium scoops vanilla bean or original vanilla ice cream (about 1 quart/24 ounces/ 680 grams), softened until just melty at the edges

MAKES ABOUT 3½ CUPS | 28 OUNCES | 850 MILLILITERS

For the lavender-infused honey Mix the honey and lavender in a small saucepan over medium-low heat and heat until the honey is fluid, about 2½ minutes. Off the heat, cover the pan and set aside to steep for 1 hour. Strain the mixture into a small bowl, pressing on the lavender to release all the honey. Cover and set aside at room temperature until ready to use (up to 5 days).

For the shake Place the milk, vanilla extract, lemon juice, and ¼ cup (85 grams) of the lavender-infused honey in a blender and blend to mix thoroughly, about 15 seconds. Add the ice cream and pulse several times to begin breaking it up. With the blender motor off, use a flexible spatula to mash the mixture down onto the blender blades. Continue pulsing, stopping, and mashing until the mixture is well blended, thick, and moves easily in the blender jar, roughly 30 to 90 seconds. Pour into a chilled glass or glasses, and serve at once.

Vanilla-Honey-Sesame Shake

When I shop in supermarkets with bulk candy departments, I have to steer a wide berth around the honey-sesame crunch bin. My love for the crunch is fierce, as it is for just about everything of the sesame persuasion, including Asian toasted sesame oil. Some of my friends grimaced when I told them I was developing a sesame shake, but I had faith, and it paid off.

The nutty sesame oil adds a subtle but alluring toasty flavor that dovetails beautifully with the sweet, floral honey. Naturally, a sprinkling of toasted sesame seeds would be the perfect garnish here.

½ cup cold whole or lowfat milk (about 4 ounces/125 milliliters)

¼ teaspoon pure vanilla extract

1½ teaspoons toasted sesame oil

2 tablespoons honey (about 1½ ounces/43 grams)

8 medium scoops vanilla bean or original vanilla ice cream (about 1 quart/24 ounces/ 680 grams), softened until just melty at the edges

MAKES ABOUT 3½ CUPS | 28 OUNCES | 850 MILLILITERS

Place the milk, vanilla extract, sesame oil, and honey in a blender and blend to mix thoroughly, about 15 seconds. Add the ice cream and pulse several times to begin breaking it up. With the blender motor off, use a flexible spatula to mash the mixture down onto the blender blades. Continue pulsing, stopping, and mashing until the mixture is well blended, thick, and moves easily in the blender jar, roughly 30 to 90 seconds. Pour into a chilled glass or glasses, and serve at once.

Frozen Affogato Shake with Espresso Granita

Affogato is an Italian stroke of genius—a quick, elegant dessert made by pouring a shot of hot espresso over a scoop of cold vanilla gelato. The espresso melts some of the gelato, creating a bittersweet, creamy sauce.

I borrowed that idea for this shake, but instead of using the hot espresso, I froze it into an icy granita with which I topped the Ballistic Vanilla Shake found on page 40. You get the classic *affogato* flavor dynamic—intense coffee playing against smooth, mellow vanilla, and the granita even adds a bit of crunch to the shake.

Granita couldn't be simpler to make. As the sweetened espresso freezes, use a dinner fork to break up the ice crystals into a loose, coffee snow. Don't substitute regular brewed coffee for the espresso; you really need that concentrated coffee flavor to counter the rich vanilla shake.

By the way, espresso granita is fabulous as a cap not just for a vanilla shake but also for either of the basic chocolate shakes (pages 42 and 44), and for the Coffee-Hazelnut (page 95), Bananas Foster (page 111), Spiced Pumpkin (page 150), Pain d'Épices (page 165), and Malted Caramel (page 175) shakes.

(Recipe on next page)

Facing page: Frozen Affogato Shake with Espresso Granita.

8 shots freshly
pulled espresso
(about 1 cup/
8 ounces/
250 milliliters), at
room temperature

5 tablespoons
sugar (about
2 1/2 ounces/60 grams)

1/2 cup cold whole or
lowfat milk (about
4 ounces/125 milliliters)

2 teaspoons pure
vanilla extract

8 medium scoops
French vanilla ice
cream (about 1 quart/
24 ounces/680 grams),
softened until just
melty at the edges

For the espresso granita Stir the espresso and sugar in a shallow container to dissolve the sugar completely. Cover and freeze until softly frozen (not solid), 2 1/2 to 3 hours. Remove from the freezer and gently run a dinner fork through the frozen mass to break it down into loose, icy crystals. Cover the container and return it to the freezer. Freeze until firm, checking and raking the granita with the fork every hour or two to keep the crystals loose and fine, at least 7 hours.

For the shake Place the milk, vanilla extract, and ice cream in a blender and pulse several times to begin breaking it up. With the blender motor off, use a flexible spatula to mash the mixture down onto the blender blades. Continue pulsing, stopping, and mashing until the mixture is well blended, thick, and moves easily in the blender jar, roughly 30 to 90 seconds. Pour into a chilled glass or glasses, top each with about 1/2 cup (about 2 1/2 ounces/70 grams) espresso granita, and serve at once.

Vanilla, Rum, and Salted Cashew Shake

When I walk into a party and spy a bowl of salted cashews, it's all I can do to stop myself from swiping the bowl, stealing off to a remote corner with it, and hissing like a threatened house cat if anyone dares to reach for a nut while I gobble them down.

Cashew butter makes it easy to harness the nuts' seductive flavor into a shake. For a cool garnish (courtesy of food stylist Michael Pederson), finely crush about ½ cup (about 3 ounces/85 grams) of salted cashews, moisten the rims of the glasses, and dip them into the crushed nuts so they adhere like the salt on the rim of a Margarita glass.

¼ cup cold whole or lowfat milk (about 2 ounces/60 milliliters)

¼ cup dark or amber rum (about 2 ounces/60 milliliters)

¼ teaspoon pure vanilla extract

6 tablespoons cashew butter (about 3 ½ ounces/100 grams)

Pinch of salt

8 medium scoops French vanilla ice cream (about 1 quart/24 ounces/ 680 grams), softened until just melty at the edges

MAKES ABOUT 3½ CUPS | 28 OUNCES | 850 MILLILITERS

Place the milk, rum, vanilla extract, cashew butter, and salt in a blender and blend to mix thoroughly, about 30 seconds. Add the ice cream and pulse several times to begin breaking it up. With the blender motor off, use a flexible spatula to mash the mixture down onto the blender blades. Continue pulsing, stopping, and mashing until the mixture is well blended, thick, and moves easily in the blender jar, roughly 30 to 90 seconds. Pour into a chilled glass or glasses, and serve at once.

VanBan Black & White Shake

I admit to taking liberties with the notion of black & white, which is commonly recognized as a shake made with chocolate syrup, the black, and vanilla ice cream, the white. Well, I couldn't shake (pun intended) the vision of New York black & white cookies; one half is frosted with chocolate fondant, and the other half with vanilla fondant. Both are present and accounted for, yet separate and distinct. So that is the route we'll take with our VanBan Black & White—separate and distinct chocolate and vanilla shakes, layered in the glass.

As if layering two flavors wasn't enough, I also give the vanilla portion of the program a little twist by adding some banana (hence the VanBan moniker), which goes so well with the chocolate. It's very helpful to have two blenders for this shake. If you don't, make one of the shakes first and store it in the refrigerator while you rush to make the second flavor.

(Recipe on next page)

Facing page: VanBan Black & White Shake.

½ cup cold whole or lowfat milk (about 4 ounces/125 milliliters)

1 ¼ teaspoons pure vanilla extract

½ ripe medium banana (2 to 3 ounces/57 to 85 grams), peeled and mashed

4 medium scoops French vanilla ice cream (about 1 pint/ 12 ounces/340 grams), softened until just melty at the edges

2 medium scoops chocolate ice cream (about ½ pint/ 6 ounces/170 grams), softened until just melty at the edges

2 medium scoops chocolate sorbet (about ½ pint/ 6 ounces/170 grams), softened until just melty at the edges

Place ¼ cup of the milk, 1 teaspoon of the vanilla extract, and the banana in a blender and blend to mix thoroughly, about 30 seconds. Add the vanilla ice cream and pulse several times to begin breaking it up. With the blender motor off, use a flexible spatula to mash the mixture down onto the blender blades. Continue pulsing, stopping, and mashing until the mixture is well blended, thick, and moves easily in the blender jar, roughly 30 to 90 seconds. Pour the shake into a small pitcher, and refrigerate while making the other flavor (if you have two blenders, keep the shake in the blender jar).

If necessary, rinse the blender jar, shake out any excess water, and return it to the base. Place the remaining ¼ cup milk, the remaining ¼ teaspoon vanilla extract, and the chocolate ice cream and sorbet in the blender and pulse several times to begin breaking up the ice cream and sorbet. With the blender motor off, use a flexible spatula to mash the mixture down onto the blender blades. Continue pulsing, stopping, and mashing until the mixture is well blended, thick, and moves easily in the blender jar, roughly 30 to 90 seconds.

Into one or two tall, chilled glasses, pour a layer of VanBan shake, followed by a layer of chocolate, another layer of VanBan, another layer of chocolate, and finishing with a last layer of VanBan on top. Serve at once.

The Original Duckfat
Vanilla Milkshake

Fear not—there is no actual fat of flying fowl involved here. Duck-fat is the name of a small, informal restaurant in Portland, Maine, with two incredible house specialties—Belgian-style fries that are, indeed, fried in duck fat, infusing the slivers of organic, local potatoes with a mind-blowing depth and richness of flavor; and extravagant milkshakes. Made with ice cream produced at the nearby Smiling Hills Farm, the Duckfat shakes are frosty, thick, and lush. The shakes were based not on the traditional combination of ice cream and milk, but on ice cream blended with crème anglaise, the classic French custard sauce made from egg yolks and cream. A more luxurious or indulgent shake is difficult to imagine!

Chef-owners Rob Evans and Nancy Pugh kindly offered me their original vanilla shake recipe. "The idea is to enhance a flavored ice cream with an intense crème anglaise" says Chef Evans, and he suggests flavor options including 1 cup of chopped fresh ginger or toasted nuts (allow the hot cream to rest with the flavoring ingredient for about 20 minutes before straining and mixing it with the yolk mixture), or ¼ cup (about 2 ounces/57 grams) of instant espresso powder. The crème anglaise recipe yields about 3 cups (about 27 ounces/765 grams) of custard, enough for three batches of milkshakes.

When you rinse the pot used to infuse the cream mixture so you can finish cooking the custard in it, don't bother to dry it. The film of water acts as extra insurance against scorching.

(Recipe on next page)

3 ¼ cups half-and-half (about 26 ounces/ 800 milliliters)

2 vanilla beans

6 egg yolks

5 tablespoons sugar (about 2 ½ ounces/60 grams)

Pinch of salt

3 medium scoops vanilla ice cream (about ¾ pint/9 ounces/ 255 grams), softened until just melty at the edges

MAKES ABOUT 2½ CUPS | 20 OUNCES | 600 MILLILITERS

For the crème anglaise Place the half-and-half in a small heavy saucepan. Using a sharp paring knife, carefully split the vanilla beans lengthwise and scrape the seeds into the cream, then add the hulls. Set the pan over medium heat and, stirring occasionally, bring the cream to a bare simmer. Off the heat, allow the cream to infuse for about 10 minutes.

Meanwhile, whisk the egg yolks, sugar, and salt in a medium, heavy, heatproof bowl until light and frothy, about 2 minutes. Secure the bowl in position by wrapping a damp kitchen towel around the base. Whisking constantly, very slowly and gradually pour the warm, infused cream into the yolk mixture until it is all incorporated.

Rinse, but don't dry, the saucepan. Pour the cream and egg mixture into the pan, set it over low heat, and cook, stirring constantly, until the mixture thickens and coats a wooden spoon to the degree that you leave a crisp-edged, clear trail when you draw your finger across the back of the spoon, about 12 minutes. Set a fine-mesh sieve over a medium bowl and strain the custard into it. Cover with a piece of plastic wrap, pressing it right onto the surface of the custard and poking several holes with the tip of a paring knife for the steam to escape. Allow the custard to cool to lukewarm and then refrigerate until well chilled, at least 4 hours and up to 4 days.

For the shake Place 1 cup (about 9 ounces/255 grams) of the chilled crème anglaise and the ice cream in a blender and pulse several times to begin breaking up the ice cream. With the blender motor off, use a flexible spatula to mash the mixture down onto the blender blades. Continue pulsing, stopping, and mashing until the mixture is well blended, thick, and moves easily in the blender jar, roughly 30 to 90 seconds. Pour into a chilled glass or glasses, and serve at once.

CHOCOLATE SHAKES

Mexican Chocolate Shake
with Chipotle and Almond

In this classic Mexican combination of chocolate, almond, cinnamon, and chile I use powdered chipotles, which are dried, smoked jalapeños. The chipotle powder imparts a subtle, smoky note that complements the chocolate, as well as a bit of heat to the finish. Chipotle powder is widely available, usually in the spice or Latin foods sections of the supermarket. You can use cayenne instead—it will give you the heat without the smoke.

½ cup cold whole or lowfat milk (about 4 ounces/125 milliliters)

¼ teaspoon almond extract

½ teaspoon ground cinnamon

⅛ teaspoon chipotle powder or cayenne pepper, or more to taste

4 medium scoops vanilla bean or original vanilla ice cream (about 1 pint/12 ounces/ 340 grams), softened until just melty at the edges

4 medium scoops chocolate sorbet (about 1 pint/ 12 ounces/340 grams), softened until just melty at the edges

MAKES ABOUT 3½ CUPS | 28 OUNCES | 850 MILLILITERS

Place the milk, almond extract, cinnamon, and chipotle in a blender and blend to mix thoroughly, about 15 seconds. Add the ice cream and sorbet and pulse several times to begin breaking them up. With the blender motor off, use a flexible spatula to mash the mixture down onto the blender blades. Continue pulsing, stopping, and mashing until the mixture is well blended, thick, and moves easily in the blender jar, roughly 30 to 90 seconds. Pour into a chilled glass or glasses, and serve at once.

Facing page: Mexican Chocolate Shake with Chipotle and Almond.

Gianduja Shake

In this shake, Nutella and Frangelico combine to re-create the chocolate-hazelnut flavor of classic Italian gianduja.

½ cup cold whole or lowfat milk (about 4 ounces/125 milliliters)

1 tablespoon Frangelico liqueur (about ½ ounce/15 milliliters)

6 tablespoons Nutella (or other chocolate-hazelnut spread; about 3 ounces/85 grams)

7 medium scoops French vanilla ice cream (about 1¾ pints/21 ounces/ 595 grams), softened until just melty at the edges

1 medium scoop chocolate sorbet (about ¼ pint/ 3 ounces/85 grams), softened until just melty at the edges

MAKES ABOUT 3½ CUPS | 28 OUNCES | 850 MILLILITERS

Place the milk, Frangelico, and Nutella in a blender and blend to mix thoroughly, about 30 seconds. Add the ice cream and sorbet and pulse several times to begin breaking them up. With the blender motor off, use a flexible spatula to mash the mixture down onto the blender blades. Continue pulsing, stopping, and mashing until the mixture is well blended, thick, and moves easily in the blender jar, roughly 30 to 90 seconds. Pour into a chilled glass or glasses, and serve at once.

Shake de l'Opéra

In 2004 I lived in Paris, which was a pleasure in more ways than I can count. Not the least of them was the incredible number of pâtisseries everywhere in the city. On our block alone there were three!

Most pâtisseries offer a traditional selection of pastries and cakes. One mainstay is *l'opéra*, or opera cake, which comprises thin sheets of almond cake soaked in coffee syrup and layered with espresso buttercream and chocolate ganache. The whole thing is covered in glistening chocolate glaze, and typically, the name *l'opéra* is written on the cake, also in chocolate, and a small shard of edible gold leaf graces the top. It's a remarkable cake, so why not make a remarkable shake with the same flavors?

Look for instant espresso powder at Italian specialty stores. Once you have a jar, you'll start using it for all things chocolate. Your brownies, especially, will never be the same.

½ cup cold whole or lowfat milk (about 4 ounces/125 milliliters)

2 ½ teaspoons instant espresso powder

½ teaspoon almond extract

4 medium scoops French vanilla ice cream (about 1 pint/ 12 ounces/340 grams), softened until just melty at the edges

4 medium scoops chocolate sorbet (about 1 pint/ 12 ounces/340 grams), softened until just melty at the edges

MAKES ABOUT 3½ CUPS | 28 OUNCES | 850 MILLILITERS

Place the milk, espresso powder, and almond extract in a blender and blend to mix thoroughly, about 15 seconds. Add the ice cream and sorbet and pulse several times to begin breaking them up. With the blender motor off, use a flexible spatula to mash the mixture down onto the blender blades. Continue pulsing, stopping, and mashing until the mixture is well blended, thick, and moves easily in the blender jar, roughly 30 to 90 seconds. Pour into a chilled glass or glasses, and serve at once.

Coconut Patty Shake

My grandparents lived in Manhattan, but in time-honored New York snowbird tradition, they spent every winter in Florida. Like clockwork each year they'd send a crate of incredible Florida oranges and grapefruit to those of us marooned up north. Without fail, packed on top of the citrus there was a long narrow box of sweet, tender, chocolate-covered coconut patties. Suffice it to say that quickly I caught on to the merits of combining chocolate and coconut.

Cream of coconut is even richer and more flavorful than coconut milk; look for it in the international aisle of the supermarket (if it's not there, it may be with the cocktail supplies—it's a standard ingredient in Piña Coladas). Even with the cream of coconut, the texture of this all-sorbet shake is slightly icy, and very refreshing. If you'd prefer it creamier and have access to coconut ice cream in your supermarket (I don't), substitute the ice cream for the coconut sorbet.

A sprinkle of lightly toasted, shredded, unsweetened coconut would be great as a garnish.

½ cup cream of coconut (such as Coco Lopez) (about 4 ounces/125 milliliters)

¼ teaspoon pure vanilla extract

6 medium scoops coconut sorbet (about 1½ pints/18 ounces/ 510 grams), softened until just melty at the edges

2 medium scoops chocolate sorbet (about ½ pint/ 6 ounces/170 grams), softened until just melty at the edges

MAKES ABOUT 3½ CUPS | 28 OUNCES | 850 MILLILITERS

Place the cream of coconut, vanilla extract, and sorbet in the blender and pulse several times to begin breaking up the sorbet. With the blender motor off, use a flexible spatula to mash the mixture down onto the blender blades. Continue pulsing, stopping, and mashing until the mixture is well blended, thick, and moves easily in the blender jar, roughly 30 to 90 seconds. Pour into a chilled glass or glasses, and serve at once.

Chocolate-Tangerine Shake

My esteemed editor at the *Boston Globe Magazine*, Anne Nelson (a cookbook author herself), called one day and said: "Adam, you won't believe this fabulous chocolate cake from Nigella Lawson I just made! You puree whole poached clementines and use them in the batter."

I believed it all right, because chocolate and orange or tangerine is a fantastic combination. This shake, bright and tangy with tangerine, may remind you of a Creamsicle, but it's better—because there is chocolate to add its earthy depth and sweetness. If you can't find tangerine sorbet, orange sorbet stands in nicely.

½ cup cold whole or lowfat milk (about 4 ounces/125 milliliters)

¼ teaspoon pure vanilla extract

4 medium scoops vanilla bean or original vanilla ice cream (about 1 pint/12 ounces/ 340 grams), softened until just melty at the edges

2 medium scoops chocolate sorbet (about ½ pint/ 6 ounces/170 grams), softened until just melty at the edges

2 medium scoops tangerine sorbet (about ½ pint/ 6 ounces/170 grams), softened until just melty at the edges

MAKES ABOUT 3½ CUPS | 28 OUNCES | 850 MILLILITERS

Place the milk, vanilla extract, ice cream, and sorbet in the blender and pulse several times to begin breaking up the ice cream and sorbet. With the blender motor off, use a flexible spatula to mash the mixture down onto the blender blades. Continue pulsing, stopping, and mashing until the mixture is well blended, thick, and moves easily in the blender jar, roughly 30 to 90 seconds. Pour into a chilled glass or glasses, and serve at once.

Chocolate-Guinness Shake

Near the climax of the Academy Award–winning 2008 movie *There Will Be Blood*, Daniel Plainview, a ruthless early twentieth-century oil driller played by Daniel Day-Lewis, maniacally bellows at his nemesis, Eli Sunday, "Here, if you have a milkshake, and I have a milkshake, and I have a straw . . . and my straw reaches across the room, and starts to drink your milkshake . . . I . . . drink . . . your . . . milkshake. I DRINK IT UP!" Like memorable lines from other famous movies—"There's no place like home," "Frankly, my dear, I don't give a damn," "Here's looking at you, kid"—Plainview's line has wormed its way into the national psyche—and vernacular.

How could I not use this as inspiration for a milkshake flavor? In collusion, the Guinness stout and chocolate sorbet give this shake a deep, malty, unusual bittersweet flavor.

(Recipe on next page)

Facing page: Chocolate-Guinness Shake.

2/3 cup Guinness stout, at room temperature (about 5 ounces/150 milliliters)

1/4 teaspoon pure vanilla extract

6 medium scoops French vanilla ice cream (about 1 1/2 pints/18 ounces/510 grams), softened until just melty at the edges

2 medium scoops chocolate sorbet (about 1/2 pint/6 ounces/170 grams), softened until just melty at the edges

Place the Guinness, vanilla extract, ice cream, and sorbet in a blender and pulse several times to begin breaking up the ice cream and sorbet. With the blender motor off, use a flexible spatula to mash the mixture down onto the blender blades. Continue pulsing, stopping, and mashing until the mixture is well blended, thick, and moves easily in the blender jar, roughly 30 to 90 seconds. Pour into a chilled glass or glasses, and serve at once.

Molasses Variation

Follow the recipe for the Chocolate-Guinness Shake, adding 1 tablespoon of molasses (about 1/2 ounce/22 grams) to the blender along with the other ingredients.

Malted Variation

Follow the recipe for the Chocolate-Guinness Shake, adding 1 tablespoon of malted milk powder (about 1/2 ounce/15 grams) to the blender with the Guinness and the vanilla extract, and blending for a moment before adding the ice cream and sorbet.

Espresso Variation

Follow the recipe for the Chocolate-Guinness Shake, adding 1 shot of room temperature espresso (about 2 tablespoons/1 ounce/30 milliliters) to the blender along with the other ingredients.

Black Forest Shake

Some people choose a different flavor of birthday cake every year, but not my friend Jonathan. He's reliable. No matter how topsy-turvy life is, Jonathan always opts for Black Forest cake, with cherries and whipped cream between layers of dark chocolate cake. Here, chocolate sorbet, cherry-vanilla ice cream, and cherry preserves combine to make a formidable shake that mimics the flavors of the cake. This one's for you, Jonathan.

MAKES ABOUT 3½ CUPS | 28 OUNCES | 850 MILLILITERS

½ cup cold cherry juice (about 4 ounces/125 milliliters)

2 tablespoons cherry preserves (about 1 ounce/28 grams)

½ teaspoon pure vanilla extract

4 medium scoops cherry-vanilla ice cream (about 1 pint/ 12 ounces/340 grams), softened until just melty at the edges

4 medium scoops chocolate sorbet (about 1 pint/ 12 ounces/340 grams), softened until just melty at the edges

Place the cherry juice, preserves, and vanilla extract in a blender and blend to mix thoroughly, about 30 seconds. Add the ice cream and sorbet and pulse several times to begin breaking them up. With the blender motor off, use a flexible spatula to mash the mixture down onto the blender blades. Continue pulsing, stopping, and mashing until the mixture is well blended, thick, and moves easily in the blender jar, roughly 30 to 90 seconds. Pour into a chilled glass or glasses, and serve at once.

Reagan Redeemed

In the staunchly Democratic household of my youth, President Ronald Reagan was known mainly for his love of jelly beans and the Iran Contra scandal. The tide might have turned had we known that he proclaimed July National Ice Cream Month, and the third Sunday in July National Ice Cream Day. Bold political move, no, but a great step toward raising national spirits.

National Ice Cream Month and National Ice Cream Day are just the tip of the iceberg when it comes to the dates recognized for ice creamy treats. June 21, for instance, is National Vanilla Milkshake Day, September 12 is National Chocolate Milkshake Day, and October 7 is National Frappe Day. For a full list, consult the Web site www.allabouticecream.com.

Spicy Chocolate Ginger Shake

One travel experience I'll never forget was the time I stumbled into the fragrant fields of fresh ginger between Brisbane and Noosa, in Queensland, Australia. Stands along the road sold ginger in every form imaginable, and it was there that I developed an addiction to crystallized (candied) ginger, which gives the sensation of sugar, fire, and ice in a single bite.

With thoughts of crystallized ginger dipped in chocolate, I developed this shake. In addition to the ginger ice cream and chocolate sorbet, a healthy dose of grated fresh ginger provides a clear, high, sweet bite to contrast the chocolate's fruity depth.

½ cup cold whole or lowfat milk (about 4 ounces/125 milliliters)

1 tablespoon finely grated fresh ginger

4 medium scoops ginger ice cream (about 1 pint/ 12 ounces/ 340 grams), softened until just melty at the edges

4 medium scoops chocolate sorbet (about 1 pint/ 12 ounces/340 grams), softened until just melty at the edges

MAKES ABOUT 3½ CUPS | 28 OUNCES | 850 MILLILITERS

Place the milk and ginger in a blender and blend to mix thoroughly, about 30 seconds. Add the ice cream and sorbet and pulse several times to begin breaking them up. With the blender motor off, use a flexible spatula to mash the mixture down onto the blender blades. Continue pulsing, stopping, and mashing until the mixture is well blended, thick, and moves easily in the blender jar, roughly 30 to 90 seconds. Pour into a chilled glass or glasses, and serve at once.

TEA AND COFFEE SHAKES

Chocolate—Earl Grey Shake

Earl Grey tea is flavored with the essence of a very sour type of orange, grown mostly in Italy, called bergamot (there is an herb with the same name, too). Despite the fact that nearly every supermarket worth its salt carries Earl Grey, I was all set to go online to my favorite tea supplier, Upton Tea Imports (www.uptontea.com) to order a batch of their special extra bergamot Earl Grey for this shake.

Well, I would have had great tea parties, but it wouldn't have been necessary for the shake. It turns out that standard supermarket Earl Grey has plenty of bergamot horsepower for the task. The fragrant, citrus-laced tea provides a subtle but captivating background flavor for a mild chocolate shake.

2/3 cup whole or lowfat milk (about 5 ounces/ 150 milliliters)

2 Earl Grey tea bags or 2 teaspoons loose tea

1/4 teaspoon pure vanilla extract

7 medium scoops vanilla bean or original vanilla ice cream (about 1 3/4 pints/ 21 ounces/595 grams), softened until just melty at the edges

1 medium scoop chocolate sorbet (about 1/4 pint/ 3 ounces/85 grams), softened until just melty at the edges

For the tea-infused milk Heat the milk in a small saucepan over medium heat, swirling the pan occasionally to help prevent scorching, until steaming, about 2 minutes. Off the heat, immerse the tea bags (or loose tea) in the milk, and steep for 4 minutes. Remove the tea bags, squeeze as much liquid as possible back into the pan, and discard them (or pour the milk through a strainer to remove loose tea leaves). Cool the milk to room temperature, cover, and refrigerate for at least 30 minutes (or up to 3 days).

For the shake Place the tea-infused milk, vanilla extract, ice cream, and sorbet in a blender and pulse several times to begin breaking up the ice cream and sorbet. With the blender motor off, use a flexible spatula to mash the mixture down onto the blender blades. Continue pulsing, stopping, and mashing until the mixture is well blended, thick, and moves easily in the blender jar, roughly 30 to 90 seconds. Pour into a chilled glass or glasses, and serve at once.

Irish Breakfast Shake

Fear not. We aren't talking about the traditional Irish breakfast of sausage, bacon, black pudding, eggs, and broiled tomatoes called an "Irish fry." (Throw in some potato bread to make it an "Ulster fry.") The flavor here is that of Irish Breakfast tea, dark, robust, and unmistakably malty.

When we shared an office at *Cook's Illustrated*, my friend Dawn Yanagihara taught me how great a flavoring tea can be. No wonder this shake was her idea. In particular, I remember being blown away by two of Dawn's tea-infused dishes—crème brûlée and jasmine tea lemon ice. This shake joins that pantheon.

2/3 cup water (about
5 ounces/150 milliliters)

4 Irish Breakfast
tea bags or
4 teaspoons loose tea

4 teaspoons
honey (about
1 ounce/28 grams)

8 medium scoops
French vanilla ice
cream (about
1 quart/24 ounces/
680 grams), softened
until just melty
at the edges

For the strong tea Bring the water to a boil in a small saucepan over high heat. Off the heat, immerse the tea bags (or loose tea) in the water, steep for 4 minutes, remove (squeeze out as much liquid as possible back into the pan), and discard (or pour the brewed tea through a strainer to remove loose tea leaves). Add the honey and stir to dissolve it. Cool to room temperature, cover, and refrigerate for at least 30 minutes (or up to 3 days).

For the shake Place the strong tea and ice cream in a blender and pulse several times to begin breaking up the ice cream. With the blender motor off, use a flexible spatula to mash the mixture down onto the blender blades. Continue pulsing, stopping, and mashing until the mixture is well blended, thick, and moves easily in the blender jar, roughly 30 to 90 seconds. Pour into a chilled glass or glasses, and serve at once.

Malted Variation

Follow the recipe for the Irish Breakfast Shake, adding 2 teaspoons (1 ounce/28 grams) of malted milk powder to the blender along with the strong tea and blending to mix them thoroughly before adding the ice cream.

Ginger-Chai Shake

Masala chai, the sweet, spicy, milky tea that most of us call simply "chai," has exploded in popularity over the last few years. I joined that bandwagon, too. With strong notes of such warm spices as cardamom, cinnamon, ginger, star anise, peppercorn, and cloves, chai is clearly a complex, exotic alternative to plain tea.

Despite the layers of flavor that come from a battalion of spices, chai is easy to make, thanks to the liquid chai concentrates that are available in almost any well-stocked supermarket. The concentrates come in several flavors; I recommend a strong variety, such as black tea, for this shake.

½ cup cold chai concentrate, preferably a black tea variety (about 4 ounces/125 milliliters)

2 teaspoons honey (about ½ ounce/15 grams)

4 medium scoops vanilla bean or original vanilla ice cream (about 1 pint/12 ounces/ 340 grams), softened until just melty at the edges

4 medium scoops ginger ice cream (about 1 pint/ 12 ounces/ 340 grams), softened until just melty at the edges

MAKES ABOUT 3½ CUPS | 28 OUNCES | 850 MILLILITERS

Place the chai concentrate and honey in a blender and blend to mix thoroughly, about 15 seconds. Add the ice cream and pulse several times to begin breaking it up. With the blender motor off, use a flexible spatula to mash the mixture down onto the blender blades. Continue pulsing, stopping, and mashing until the mixture is well blended, thick, and moves easily in the blender jar, roughly 30 to 90 seconds. Pour into a chilled glass or glasses, and serve at once.

New England Nomenclature

At the advent of the milkshake age about a hundred years ago, milkshakes were, quite literally, milk shaken with flavoring or thickening ingredients, and very often some whiskey, too. Generally, there was no ice cream involved until roughly the 1920s. Eventually, ice cream became such a standard component of milkshakes that it came to define the drink. To most everyone in the United States, a milkshake is, simply put, ice cream, milk, and flavorings all whipped up together.

But not in New England. Though New Englanders are often quick to embrace new technology and progress, in matters of the milkshake they cling tenaciously to the old-fashioned definition of milk and flavoring syrup shaken to a froth. When ice cream enters the equation, the drink becomes a "frappe" (or, perhaps also a "velvet," as I have heard it is called in some parts of New England; I still haven't encountered a velvet firsthand, though).

Whatever the reason for the throwback nomenclature, pity the uninformed out-of-state visitors to New England who order a milkshake for the first time, thinking they will get what most of the country knows to be a milkshake; they are in for a rude, ice cream-less surprise.

To complicate matters more, if our hapless visitors happen to be in Rhode Island or adjacent southeastern Massachusetts, they're in for even more confusion. There, and there alone, the drink with milk, flavorings, and ice cream is called a "cabinet," owing, popular opinion has it, to the fact that the machines used to blend the drinks, and often the syrups used to flavor them, were kept in wooden cabinets.

Café Blanco y Negro Shake

Blanco y negro . . . white and black.

Okay, in this case, yellow—the lemon, an oft-used espresso garnish, and black—star anise. And cinnamon, for good measure. The trio permeates this light coffee shake with an almost wraithlike, point-counterpoint of flavor and fragrance. The lemon provides an aromatic high note, opposing the vaguely mentholated warmth and perfume of the anise and cinnamon. The original *café blanco y negro* is a Spanish cold coffee drink, also served with ice cream, but not typically blended into a shake.

2 tablespoons
sugar (about
1 ounce/24 grams)

Zest from 1 medium
lemon, peeled off
in thin strips

3 whole star anise

3 four-inch (ten-
centimeter)
cinnamon sticks

2/3 cup cold whole or
lowfat milk (about
5 ounces/150 milliliters)

4 medium scoops
vanilla bean or original
vanilla ice cream (about
1 pint/12 ounces/
340 grams), softened
until just melty
at the edges

4 medium scoops
coffee ice cream (about
1 pint/12 ounces/
340 grams), softened
until just melty
at the edges

MAKES ABOUT 3 1/2 CUPS | 28 OUNCES | 850 MILLILITERS

For the spice-infused milk Place the sugar and lemon zest in a small saucepan and stir them together until the sugar is moist and fragrant. Add the star anise, cinnamon sticks, and milk, set the pan over medium heat, and heat the milk, swirling the pan occasionally to help prevent scorching, until steaming, about 2 minutes. Off the heat, steep the milk and flavorings until fragrant, about 1 hour. Strain the milk, discard the solids, cover, and refrigerate for at least 30 minutes (or up to 3 days).

For the shake Place the infused milk and the ice cream in a blender and pulse several times to begin breaking up the ice cream. With the blender motor off, use a flexible spatula to mash the mixture down onto the blender blades. Continue pulsing, stopping, and mashing until the mixture is well blended, thick, and moves easily in the blender jar, roughly 30 to 90 seconds. Pour into a chilled glass or glasses, and serve at once.

Caffè Corretto Shake

I still have much of the world left to see, but of the places to which I have traveled so far, Italy has the best coffee. The espresso there is deep and bittersweet, with a flavor as smooth and intense as the Italians are passionate.

With *caffè corretto*, they gild the lily by "correcting" the espresso with a shot of liquor, usually brandy, Sambuca, or, for the really hard-core, grappa, a firewater distilled from the skins of grapes.

¼ cup cold whole or lowfat milk (about 2 ounces/60 milliliters)

2 tablespoons brandy, cognac, or Sambuca (about 1 ounce/30 milliliters)

2 shots freshly pulled espresso, at room temperature (4 tablespoons/ 2 ounces/60 milliliters)

8 medium scoops coffee ice cream (about 1 quart/24 ounces/ 680 grams), softened until just melty at the edges

MAKES ABOUT 3½ CUPS | 28 OUNCES | 850 MILLILITERS

Place the milk, brandy, espresso, and ice cream in a blender and pulse several times to begin breaking up the ice cream. With the blender motor off, use a flexible spatula to mash the mixture down onto the blender blades. Continue pulsing, stopping, and mashing until the mixture is well blended, thick, and moves easily in the blender jar, roughly 30 to 90 seconds. Pour into a chilled glass or glasses, and serve at once.

Coffee- and Cabinet-Crazed Rhode Island

Rhode Island is a small state with a big love for all things coffee. While most of the country gulps down chocolate milk, that familiar childhood (and adulthood, for that matter) treat of milk flavored with chocolate syrup or powder, Rhode Islanders have their own version—coffee milk. Throughout the state, and in adjacent southeastern Massachusetts, coffee syrup is the standard flavoring for milk. On the shelves of area supermarkets, it sits right next to the chocolate syrup. In 1993 the Rhode Island legislature cemented the position of coffee milk in state history by proclaiming it to be the official state drink.

Rhode Island's love affair with coffee doesn't stop there. The state is also thought to lead the country in per capita consumption of coffee ice cream. And where there is ice cream, there have to be milkshakes, right?

Guess again. When Rhode Islanders blend coffee ice cream with coffee milk, the result—what most of us would consider to be a milkshake (or in the rest of New England, a frappe)—is called a coffee cabinet.

Supremacy in the world of Rhode Island coffee syrups is a matter of considerable debate. Three top brands, Autocrat, Eclipse, and Coffee Time, all made locally in Rhode Island, of course, have passionate devotees. Generally, Autocrat is considered to be the sweetest of the three; Eclipse and Coffee Time are thought to have a stronger coffee flavor. Now all three syrups are produced in Lincoln, Rhode Island, by Autocrat, Inc., a company that dates back to 1895. To purchase coffee syrup online, go to www.autocrat.com/cart, and with your new bottle of syrup in hand, make a Rhode Island coffee cabinet at home using the following recipe.

Rhode Island Coffee Cabinet

A coffee cabinet just isn't a coffee cabinet without coffee syrup. Your cabinet will have a slightly stronger flavor if you use Eclipse or Coffee Time syrup, as opposed to Autocrat. Autocrat, however, should win a design award for its elegant packaging and labeling.

½ cup cold whole or lowfat milk (about 4 ounces/125 milliliters)

¼ cup coffee syrup (about 2 ounces/ 60 milliliters)

8 medium scoops coffee ice cream (about 1 quart/24 ounces/ 680 grams), softened until just melty at the edges

MAKES ABOUT 3½ CUPS | 28 OUNCES | 850 MILLILITERS

Place the milk, syrup, and ice cream in a blender and pulse several times to begin breaking up the ice cream. With the blender motor off, use a flexible spatula to mash the mixture down onto the blender blades. Continue pulsing, stopping, and mashing until the mixture is well blended, thick, and moves easily in the blender jar, roughly 30 to 90 seconds. Pour into a chilled glass or glasses, and serve at once.

Facing page: Rhode Island Coffee Cabinet.

Vietnamese Iced Coffee Shake

Whether it is hot or iced, Vietnamese coffee is distinctive in several ways. First, it is mixed with sweetened condensed milk, probably because fresh dairy products didn't keep so well in the tropical heat before refrigeration became common. In fact, the coffee is usually brewed right into the same glass with the sweetened condensed milk. Second, the brew is made with coarsely ground, dark-roasted coffee, very often French roast or French roast with chicory.

Last is the means by which the coffee is made—in a single serving press, called a *phin*, that sits right over the glass. Many writers note that it resembles a small, stainless steel top hat—a pretty apt description. The press has a brim that holds it on the rim of the glass, with a cylindrical chamber above the brim for coffee grounds and hot water. The coffee grounds are compressed between two metal filters in that chamber, and the compression pressure controls the water flow speed and the strength of the brew. Some Vietnamese restaurants present the whole assembly when you order coffee. I have seen the presses for sale in Asian markets in many cities, or online at www.trung-nguyen-online.com and www.asianfoodgrocer.com.

It's an interesting process to behold, but for this shake it's sort of a moot point. Once the coffee and sweetened condensed milk are mixed, Vietnamese iced coffee has a relatively light coffee flavor, and a pronounced sweetness from the milk. So the coffee ice cream provides all the java flavor you need here. Kind of ironic, isn't it?

In his book *The Perfect Scoop* (Ten Speed Press, 2007), author, blogger, and friend David Lebovitz adds a pinch of finely ground coffee to his recipe for Vietnamese coffee ice cream; you can do the same in this shake, as well.

½ cup regular or lowfat sweetened condensed milk (about 4 ounces/ 125 milliliters)

8 medium scoops coffee ice cream (about 1 quart/24 ounces/ 680 grams), softened until just melty at the edges

Place the sweetened condensed milk and ice cream in a blender and pulse several times to begin breaking up the ice cream. With the blender motor off, use a flexible spatula to mash the mixture down onto the blender blades. Continue pulsing, stopping, and mashing until the mixture is well blended, thick, and moves easily in the blender jar, roughly 30 to 90 seconds. Pour into a chilled glass or glasses, and serve at once.

Coffee Syrup and the Good Ol' Days

When it came time to study up on coffee syrup, coffee milk, and cabinets, my first call was to my good friend Elizabeth. Her credentials on the topic are impeccable. Not only is she a librarian by trade (so no piece of information eludes her), but she knows the subject from lifelong experience because she grew up in the southeastern Massachusetts city of Fall River, a stone's throw from the Rhode Island border.

After she vigorously defended Autocrat coffee syrup as her brand of choice, I asked if there were any particular coffee milk rituals in her family. "Well, let's see," she said, "there was the eggnog in the morning, and—" I stopped her. "No, no, I was asking about coffee milk, not eggnog," I said. "I know," she replied, "the eggnog was made with coffee milk." I learned that when Elizabeth was a little girl in the late 1960s, a standard school-day breakfast for her and her seven brothers was a mixture of milk, coffee syrup, and raw eggs, whipped to a froth in the blender.

We confirmed Elizabeth's memory with her mother, Cornelia. "Sure," she said, "all the mothers made that for their kids' breakfasts. Our pediatrician recommended it, for the protein." Clearly, back in the 1960s there wasn't the same worry about eating raw eggs as there is today. Cornelia acknowledged the difference in the times, too, and then added, with a wisp of nostalgia for simpler times, ". . . but the kids all came out fine. As long as you don't look too hard."

Coffee-Hazelnut Shake

Spending time in the Northwest, an area rife with hazelnuts (or fil-berts, in the local parlance), locks them into your taste conscious-ness. I use the nuts in cakes, tarts, cookies, bars, and even salad dressing, in the guise of hazelnut oil. They were a little too coarse for a shake, though, so enter Frangelico, an Italian hazelnut-based liqueur. The espresso powder adds more coffee kick.

¼ cup cold whole or lowfat milk (about 2 ounces/60 milliliters)

¼ cup Frangelico liqueur (about 2 ounces/60 milliliters)

2 ½ teaspoons instant espresso powder

8 medium scoops coffee ice cream (about 1 quart/24 ounces/ 680 grams), softened until just melty at the edges

MAKES ABOUT 3½ CUPS | 28 OUNCES | 850 MILLILITERS

Place the milk, Frangelico, and espresso pow-der in a blender and blend to mix thoroughly, about 15 seconds. Add the ice cream and pulse several times to begin breaking it up. With the blender motor off, use a flexible spatula to mash the mixture down onto the blender blades. Continue pulsing, stopping, and mashing until the mixture is well blended, thick, and moves easily in the blender jar, roughly 30 to 90 sec-onds. Pour into a chilled glass or glasses, and serve at once.

Mocha-Cardamom Shake

I am head over heels for cardamom, with its intoxicating sweet-spicy aroma and delicate notes of lemon and pepper. Perhaps the most seductive of all the spices, cardamom provides a vaguely exotic and truly remarkable accent to coffee. A little bit of cardamom goes a long way, but do make sure your supply is fresh.

½ cup cold whole or lowfat milk (about 4 ounces/125 milliliters)

2 teaspoons instant espresso powder

¼ teaspoon ground cardamom

4 medium scoops coffee ice cream (about 1 pint/12 ounces/ 340 grams), softened until just melty at the edges

4 medium scoops chocolate sorbet (about 1 pint/ 12 ounces/340 grams), softened until just melty at the edges

MAKES ABOUT 3½ CUPS | 28 OUNCES | 850 MILLILITERS

Place the milk, espresso powder, and cardamom in a blender and blend to mix thoroughly, about 15 seconds. Add the ice cream and sorbet and pulse several times to begin breaking them up. With the blender motor off, use a flexible spatula to mash the mixture down onto the blender blades. Continue pulsing, stopping, and mashing until the mixture is well blended, thick, and moves easily in the blender jar, roughly 30 to 90 seconds. Pour into a chilled glass or glasses, and serve at once.

Facing page: Mocha-Cardamom Shake.

Awful Awful Cabinets

I'd wager that few Rhode Islanders can think of cabinets without thinking also of the Newport Creamery chain of ice cream parlor/restaurants (www.newportcreamery.com). With eleven locations throughout Rhode Island, and two in neighboring southeastern Massachusetts, Newport Creamery may be best known for its signature cabinets, called Awful Awfuls.

The name derives from the catchphrase "Awful Big, Awful Good," which, according to the Newport Creamery Web site, was coined originally in the 1940s by Bond's Ice Cream in New Jersey. Samuel Rector and his son Mason, the founders of Newport Creamery, worked out a deal with Bond's to use the "Awful Awful" name. When Bond's went belly-up in the 1970s, Newport Creamery bought the name outright. Whichever flavor you choose, Awful Awfuls come with a deal—if you can drink three, you get a fourth for free.

Dead Eye Mocha Shake

After the clubs and bars close for the night in Provincetown, the beachy paradise at the very tip of Cape Cod, it seems like everyone in town congregates at Spiritus Pizza to satisfy their late-night appetites. Pizza, coffee, and ice cream are the mainstays at Spiritus, and their mocha shake, which is nothing short of extravagant, is the inspiration for this one. I named it the Dead Eye after the fashion of the coffee-fueled Pacific Northwest, where three shots of espresso in a cup of brewed coffee often goes by that name. One of these is sure to keep you up and partying until the sun rises.

6 shots freshly pulled espresso, at room temperature (12 tablespoons/ 6 ounces/180 milliliters)

6 medium scoops coffee ice cream (about 1 1/2 pints/ 18 ounces/510 grams), softened until just melty at the edges

2 medium scoops chocolate sorbet (about 1/2 pint/ 6 ounces/170 grams), softened until just melty at the edges

MAKES ABOUT 3 1/2 CUPS | 28 OUNCES | 850 MILLILITERS

Place the espresso, ice cream, and sorbet in a blender and pulse several times to begin breaking up the ice cream and sorbet. With the blender motor off, use a flexible spatula to mash the mixture down onto the blender blades. Continue pulsing, stopping, and mashing until the mixture is well blended, thick, and moves easily in the blender jar, roughly 30 to 90 seconds. Pour into a chilled glass or glasses, and serve at once.

FRUITY SHAKES

Strawberry-Basil Shake

Infusing a syrup with basil, rather than using the herb right in the shake, provides a round basil flavor with a little extra pluck from the acidity of the white wine. Choose a crisp wine that has not been aged in oak—perhaps a Sauvignon Blanc.

6 tablespoons sugar (about 3 ounces/72 grams)

2/3 cup dry white wine (about 5 ounces/150 milliliters)

1 cup (packed) fresh basil leaves, roughly chopped (about 2 ounces/57 grams)

1/4 cup cold whole or lowfat milk (about 2 ounces/60 milliliters)

4 medium scoops strawberry ice cream (about 1 pint/ 12 ounces/340 grams), softened until just melty at the edges

4 medium scoops strawberry sorbet (about 1 pint/ 12 ounces/340 grams), softened until just melty at the edges

MAKES ABOUT 3 1/2 CUPS | 28 OUNCES | 850 MILLILITERS

For the basil syrup Mix the sugar and wine in a small saucepan over medium heat, swirling the pan occasionally to dissolve the sugar. Bring the mixture to a gentle boil, reduce the heat to medium-low, and simmer for 3 minutes. Off the heat, add the chopped basil, and stir to immerse it in the liquid. Cover the pan and set aside to steep for 1 hour. Strain the syrup into a small bowl, pressing on the basil to release all the liquid, cover, and refrigerate for at least 30 minutes (or up to 3 days).

For the shake Place 1/4 cup (60 milliliters) of the chilled basil syrup, the milk, ice cream, and sorbet in a blender and pulse several times to begin breaking up the ice cream and sorbet. With the blender motor off, use a flexible spatula to mash the mixture down onto the blender blades. Continue pulsing, stopping, and mashing until the mixture is well blended, thick, and moves easily in the blender jar, roughly 30 to 90 seconds. Pour into a chilled glass or glasses, and serve at once.

Strawberry-Rhubarb Shake

In Afton, Minnesota, a historic town just east of St. Paul on the St. Croix River, June is Strawberry Festival time. It's a classic small-town shindig, with a church-sponsored pancake breakfast, games, rides, a local business "expo," police and fire equipment demonstrations, bingo, bands, and, of course, local strawberries. Loads of them. In shortcakes, ice cream, sundaes, jam, mousse, and pie. Pie after pie, after pie, after pie. The first year I went, strawberry-rhubarb was the standout among the pies—I still remember it twenty years later. And if it made that good a pie back then, why not a great shake now?

2 medium stalks rhubarb (about 8 ounces/227 grams), washed and cut into small chunks

5 tablespoons sugar (about 2 ½ ounces/60 grams)

1 tablespoon water (about ½ ounce/ 15 milliliters)

Pinch of salt

¼ cup cold whole or lowfat milk (about 2 ounces/60 milliliters)

6 medium scoops vanilla bean or original vanilla ice cream (about 1 ½ pints/ 18 ounces/510 grams), softened until just melty at the edges

2 medium scoops strawberry sorbet (about ½ pint/ 6 ounces/170 grams), softened until just melty at the edges

MAKES ABOUT 3½ CUPS | 28 OUNCES | 850 MILLILITERS

For the rhubarb Mix the rhubarb, sugar, water, and salt in a small saucepan over medium heat. Bring the mixture to a gentle boil, stirring occasionally; reduce the heat to medium-low, and simmer until the rhubarb breaks down to a coarse puree, about 20 minutes. Off the heat, cool the mixture to room temperature, then cover and refrigerate for at least 30 minutes (or up to 3 days).

For the shake Place the milk and 6 tablespoons of the rhubarb in a blender and blend to mix thoroughly, about a minute. Add the ice cream and sorbet and pulse several times to begin breaking them up. With the blender motor off, use a flexible spatula to mash the mixture down onto the blender blades. Continue pulsing, stopping, and mashing until the mixture is well blended, thick, and moves easily in the blender jar, roughly 30 to 90 seconds. Pour into a chilled glass or glasses, and serve at once.

Raspberry-Rose Shake

In Watertown, Massachusetts, a few miles from where I live, there are a number of Armenian-run markets and bakeries serving the thriving Armenian population there. My favorite among them, Sevan Bakery, has incredible *dolma* (stuffed grape leaves), *muhumara* (roasted pepper and walnut spread, often spiked with pomegranate molasses), *lamejun* (Armenian flatbreads, with or without savory toppings), feta cheese from five or six countries, a vast selection of gorgeous, glistening olives, and the most beautiful dried fruit and nuts I've seen anywhere.

It's also where I buy rose water, a common flavoring in crisp, nutty pastries and other sweets from the Middle East, North Africa, and India. Packing the powerful perfume of the petals from which it's made, rose water gives a fragrant lift to the sweet-tart raspberries in this shake. Use it sparingly, though, as you would any flavor extract; a little rose water has a lot of impact.

In case you can't make it to Sevan, look for rose water in the international aisle or with the other flavorings and extracts at well-stocked supermarkets, or online at www.kalustyans.com.

½ cup cold whole or lowfat milk (about 4 ounces/125 milliliters)

½ teaspoon rose water

2 medium scoops vanilla bean or original vanilla ice cream (about ½ pint/6 ounces/170 grams), softened until just melty at the edges

6 medium scoops raspberry sorbet (about 1 ½ pints/18 ounces/510 grams), softened until just melty at the edges

½ cup fresh raspberries (about 3 ounces/85 grams)

MAKES ABOUT 3½ CUPS | 28 OUNCES | 850 MILLILITERS

Place the milk, rose water, ice cream, and sorbet in a blender and pulse several times to begin breaking up the ice cream and sorbet. With the blender motor off, use a flexible spatula to mash the mixture down onto the blender blades. Continue pulsing, stopping, and mashing until the mixture is well blended, thick, and moves easily in the blender jar, roughly 30 to 90 seconds. Add the raspberries and pulse several times to distribute but not thoroughly integrate them. Pour into a chilled glass or glasses, and serve at once.

Blackberry-Lavender Shake

Lavender suffers from something of a misconception. Often thought of as a demure flavor with a subtle presence, its perfume is as rich as its purple color is brilliant, and the combination is actually strong enough to roll right over many of the ingredients with which it is paired.

My sister Amanda, who has spent years living in the path of encroaching blackberry bushes in the Pacific Northwest, pointed out that if any berry can stand its ground in a shake with lavender, it's the blackberry. Sweet, intense, and almost winey, blackberries can also be a force to reckon with. In this shake the blackberries and lavender temper each other's forceful personalities, resulting in a deep, complex, flowery, and nicely balanced overall flavor. If you want, reserve a few small lavender leaves to use for a beautiful purple-on-purple garnish.

(Recipe on next page)

2 1/2 cups fresh or frozen and thawed blackberries (about 12 ounces/340 grams)

6 tablespoons sugar (about 3 ounces/72 grams)

Pinch of salt

2 tablespoons water (about 1 ounce/ 30 milliliters)

3 tablespoons fresh or dried lavender flowers (about 1/4 ounce/7 grams)

2 teaspoons freshly squeezed lemon juice

4 medium scoops vanilla bean or original vanilla ice cream (about 1 pint/12 ounces/ 340 grams), softened until just melty at the edges

4 medium scoops blackberry sorbet (about 1 pint/ 12 ounces/340 grams), softened until just melty at the edges

For the lavender-infused blackberry coulis Reserve 1/2 cup (68 grams) of blackberries in a small bowl, cover, and refrigerate until ready to use. Place the remaining 2 cups (272 grams) of blackberries, the sugar, salt, and water in a food processor and process to a liquidy puree. In a small saucepan, bring the puree to a simmer over medium heat, and cook, stirring occasionally, for about 3 minutes. Off the heat, stir in the lavender, cover the pan, and set aside to steep for 1 hour. Strain the mixture into a small bowl, pressing on the solids to release as much liquid as possible (you should have about 3/4 cup/180 milliliters). Add 1/2 teaspoon of the lemon juice, cover, and refrigerate until ready to use (or up to 3 days).

For the shake Place 6 tablespoons of the blackberry-lavender coulis, the remaining 1 1/2 teaspoons lemon juice, the ice cream, and sorbet in a blender and pulse several times to begin breaking up the ice cream and sorbet. With the blender motor off, use a flexible spatula to mash the mixture down onto the blender blades. Continue pulsing, stopping, and mashing until the mixture is well blended, thick, and moves easily in the blender jar, roughly 30 to 90 seconds. Add the reserved blackberries and pulse several times to distribute but not thoroughly integrate them. Pour into a chilled glass or glasses, and serve at once.

Fresh Fig Shake

Until I was a teenager I had no idea that figs came in any form other than Newtons. The summer I was thirteen, I went shopping with my sister Amanda at the Wholesale Produce Market, near where she lived in the Bernal Heights neighborhood of San Francisco. She bought a tray of fresh figs, and when I bit into one I stopped dead in my tracks. Sweet, tender, honeyed, and floral, this fig was no Newton!

In addition to their singular flavor, figs also lend their lush texture to this uniquely velvety shake. Using a dark-skinned variety such as Black Mission imparts a lovely purple color, as well. Make this shake in the height of fig season—midsummer through early fall.

½ cup cold whole or lowfat milk (about 4 ounces/125 milliliters)

¼ teaspoon pure vanilla extract

¼ teaspoon freshly squeezed lemon juice

10 medium, fresh figs (about 12 ounces/ 340 grams), preferably Black Mission, stems removed, and halved

7 medium scoops vanilla bean or original vanilla ice cream (about 1 ¾ pints/21 ounces/ 595 grams), softened until just melty at the edges

MAKES ABOUT 3 ½ CUPS | 28 OUNCES | 850 MILLILITERS

Place the milk, vanilla extract, lemon juice, and figs in a blender and blend to break down the figs and mix thoroughly, about 30 seconds. Add the ice cream and pulse several times to begin breaking it up. With the blender motor off, use a flexible spatula to mash the mixture down onto the blender blades. Continue pulsing, stopping, and mashing until the mixture is well blended, thick, and moves easily in the blender jar, roughly 30 to 90 seconds. Pour into a chilled glass or glasses, and serve at once.

(Recipe continues on next page)

Fresh Fig and Tarragon Variation

White vermouth is infused with herbs, so it accentuates the flavor of the tarragon nicely.

5 tablespoons sugar (about 2 ½ ounces/60 grams)

¼ cup white vermouth or dry white wine (about 2 ounces/ 60 milliliters)

¼ cup water (about 2 ounces/60 milliliters)

6 tablespoons chopped fresh tarragon, plus 2 small sprigs for garnish, if desired (about 1 ½ ounces/ 43 grams)

Mix the sugar, vermouth, and water in a small saucepan set over medium heat, swirling the pan to dissolve the sugar. Bring the mixture to a gentle boil, reduce the heat to medium-low, and simmer for 3 minutes. Off the heat, add the tarragon, and stir to immerse it in the liquid. Cover the pan and set aside to steep for 1 hour. Strain the syrup into a small bowl, pressing on the tarragon to release all the liquid, cover, and refrigerate for at least 30 minutes (or up to 5 days).

Follow the recipe for the Fresh Fig Shake, substituting 6 tablespoons of the tarragon syrup for ¼ cup (60 milliliters) of the milk.

Pineapple, Ginger, and Lime Shake

If I am feeling rushed or lazy about cutting vegetables or fruit for dinner, I go shopping at a fancy supermarket salad bar, where everything I could want is prepped, pristine, and waiting. Many markets also have packaged, cut fresh fruit, including pineapple, in the refrigerated bins in the produce department. In my opinion, both routes are preferable to the canned option. Regardless of the source, choose very juicy pineapple. That way, you can strain the fruit's own juice to use in the shake, rather than buying extra.

The ginger flavor here is nice and gentle, since it comes from the ice cream alone. For extra sharpness, should you want it, add up to 2 teaspoons of grated fresh ginger along with the juice and the fruit.

¼ cup pineapple juice (about 2 ounces/60 milliliters)

3 tablespoons freshly squeezed lime juice (about 1½ ounces/ 45 milliliters)

½ cup finely chopped fresh pineapple, drained (about 4 ounces/112 grams)

4 medium scoops vanilla bean or original vanilla ice cream (about 1 pint/12 ounces/340 grams), softened until just melty at the edges

4 medium scoops ginger ice cream (about 1 pint/12 ounces/340 grams), softened until just melty at the edges

MAKES ABOUT 3½ CUPS | 28 OUNCES | 850 MILLILITERS

Place the pineapple juice, lime juice, and pineapple in a blender and blend to break down the pineapple and mix thoroughly, about 30 seconds. Add the ice cream and pulse several times to begin breaking it up. With the blender motor off, use a flexible spatula to mash the mixture down onto the blender blades. Continue pulsing, stopping, and mashing until the mixture is well blended, thick, and moves easily in the blender jar, roughly 30 to 90 seconds. Pour into a chilled glass or glasses, and serve at once.

Bananas Foster Shake

Developed at Brennan's Restaurant for a favored customer, Mr. Foster, fresh bananas sautéed in butter and brown sugar, gently spiced with cinnamon, doused with rum and flamed dramatically, and served with vanilla ice cream is a classic dessert from New Orleans. Since ice cream is part of the program already, I figured it was just one blender away from a shake.

Since the bananas end up in a puree it doesn't matter if they are a little overripe when you start. Steer clear of green-tinted underripe bananas, though, because they won't be quite as sweet as they should be. If you'd like, reserve a slice or two of the cooked banana to garnish the shakes, and a dollop of whipped cream couldn't hurt, either.

To make a Pineapple Foster Shake, substitute 2 cups fresh pineapple chunks (about 16 ounces/454 grams), well drained, for the banana and increase the cooking time to 5 minutes (the pineapple will look dry and very, very lightly browned).

(Recipe on next page)
Facing page: Bananas Foster Shake.

1½ tablespoons unsalted butter (about ¾ ounce/22 grams)

1 large banana, sliced (about 6 ounces/170 grams)

3 tablespoons light brown sugar (about 1½ ounces/38 grams)

¼ cup dark or amber rum (about 2 ounces/60 milliliters)

Pinch of ground cinnamon

⅓ cup cold whole or lowfat milk (about 2½ ounces/ 75 milliliters)

8 medium scoops French vanilla ice cream (about 1 quart/24 ounces/ 680 grams), softened until just melty at the edges

For the bananas Melt the butter in a medium nonstick skillet over medium heat and heat until it stops foaming. Add the bananas and brown sugar, stir to help melt the sugar and coat the bananas, and cook, stirring occasionally, until the bananas are soft and saucy, about 2 minutes. Add 3 tablespoons (1½ ounces/45 milliliters) of the rum, allow it to warm for a few seconds, and carefully wave a lit chimney match over the pan until the rum ignites. Allow the rum to burn until it extinguishes, about 30 seconds. Off the heat, add the cinnamon, stir to combine, and allow the mixture to cool to room temperature, about 20 minutes.

For the shake Place the bananas, sauce, milk, and remaining 1 tablespoon (½ ounce/15 milliliters) of rum in a blender and blend to mix thoroughly, about 30 seconds. Add the ice cream and pulse several times to begin breaking it up. With the blender motor off, use a flexible spatula to mash the mixture down onto the blender blades. Continue pulsing, stopping, and mashing until the mixture is well blended, thick, and moves easily in the blender jar, roughly 30 to 90 seconds. Pour into a chilled glass or glasses, and serve at once.

Avocado, Coconut, and Lime Shake

For ten years I worked as an editor at *Cook's Illustrated* magazine, which could rightly have been named *The Journal of Obsessive Recipe Testing* instead. If *Cook's* is known for anything, it is exhaustive recipe development. Test cooks there try each dish in every conceivable way, no matter how common or absurd; for that I will gladly vouch.

Sometimes, when I had finished developing a recipe for the magazine, I never wanted to see that food again—to wit, I can't remember the last time I made a stuffed pork roast. But that wasn't the case when I worked on guacamole. Even sixty batches into the project, I was always ready for more. And I still am today. There is no such thing as too much avocado.

This shake's roots are in Southeast Asia, where avocado shakes are very popular (as they are in Brazil, as well). Sweetened condensed milk is often added, but I chose to play off the avocado's tropical nature and combine it with coconut and lime. Neither flavor is assertive, though. In fact, you could go so far as to call them sneaky, with the avocado showing up in the nose and the coconut in the finish. Definitely use dark, rough-skinned Hass avocados—they are denser and silkier than the larger, brighter green variety found in many supermarkets.

If you'd like, squirt some lime juice on a couple of the avocado slices (to prevent them from discoloring) and reserve them to use as a garnish.

(Recipe on next page)

½ cup cold
coconut milk (about
4 ounces/125 milliliters)

¼ cup freshly
squeezed lime juice
(about 2 ounces/
60 milliliters)

1 ripe, small avocado
(7 to 8 ounces/198 to
227 grams), preferably
Hass, pitted, peeled,
and flesh cut into
slices, 4 thin slices
squirted with lime
juice and reserved for
garnish, if desired

8 medium scoops
coconut sorbet (about
1 quart/24 ounces/
680 grams), softened
until just melty
at the edges

MAKES ABOUT 3½ CUPS | 28 OUNCES | 850 MILLILITERS

Place the coconut milk, lime juice, and avocado in a blender and blend to mix thoroughly, about 30 seconds. Add the sorbet and pulse several times to begin breaking it up. With the blender motor off, use a flexible spatula to mash the mixture down onto the blender blades. Continue pulsing, stopping, and mashing until the mixture is well blended, thick, and moves easily in the blender jar, roughly 30 to 90 seconds. Pour into a chilled glass or glasses, and serve at once.

Mango, Chile, and Lime Shake

Everywhere you look in L.A. (and in Mexico, for that matter) there are street carts, often with signs reading "Fruta Fresca," that sell bags of cut fresh fruit sprinkled with lime juice, chile powder, and salt. The options usually include some or all of the following: watermelon, cantaloupe, honeydew, orange, pineapple, mango, papaya, coconut, cucumber, and jicama. My brother Josh, who has spent lots of time traveling around Mexico, and I both find the combination of sweet, refreshing fruit, spicy chile, and tart lime to be pretty addictive, so when he suggested a "Mexican street fruit" shake for the book, I grabbed a container of mango sorbet and got to work immediately.

¼ cup cold whole or lowfat milk (about 2 ounces/60 milliliters)

¼ cup freshly squeezed lime juice (about 2 ounces/ 60 milliliters)

¼ teaspoon pure chile powder or cayenne pepper, or to taste

Pinch of salt

4 medium scoops vanilla bean or original vanilla ice cream (about 1 pint/12 ounces/ 340 grams), softened until just melty at the edges

4 medium scoops mango sorbet (about 1 pint/12 ounces/ 340 grams), softened until just melty at the edges

Pure chile powder, which is made by grinding a single type of chile, is preferable to standard supermarket chile powder, which often contains additional spices such as cumin. Failing that, cayenne pepper will provide the necessary heat. Many street vendors seem to go heavy on the salt, but I like just enough to bring up the flavor of the mango without an overwhelming salty hit.

MAKES ABOUT 3½ CUPS | 28 OUNCES | 850 MILLILITERS

Place the milk, lime juice, chile powder, salt, ice cream, and sorbet in a blender and pulse several times to begin breaking up the ice cream and sorbet. With the blender motor off, use a flexible spatula to mash the mixture down onto the blender blades. Continue pulsing, stopping, and mashing until the mixture is well blended, thick, and moves easily in the blender jar, roughly 30 to 90 seconds. Pour into a chilled glass or glasses, and serve at once.

Sweet Guava and Crème Fraîche Shake

Guava, also called *guayaba* or *guyava*, is a fist-sized tropical fruit with a lush, sweet aroma and flavor. Guava paste, the pulp of the fruit cooked down with sugar, pectin, and citric acid to the point where it is firm enough to slice once it has cooled, might be considered a staple in Latin American countries. Guava paste swings both ways, accompanying both sweet and savory morsels with equal élan.

In this shake, guava paste is paired with rich, gently tart crème fraîche to get a satisfying sweet-tangy dynamic going on. The combination also gives the shake an incredibly thick, velvety texture. If you don't live near a market that stocks Latin American products, you can buy guava paste online at http://goya.elsstore.com. You'll probably have some left over; slice it thin and try it with thin slices of cheese, dabs of cream cheese, or slivers of ham or salami.

2/3 cup cold whole or
lowfat milk (about
5 ounces/150 milliliters)

1/2 cup guava paste
(about 5 ounces/
142 grams)

1/2 cup crème fraîche
(about 3 ounces/
85 grams)

7 medium scoops
vanilla bean or original
vanilla ice cream
(about 1 3/4 pints/
21 ounces/ 595 grams),
softened until just
melty at the edges

MAKES ABOUT 3 1/2 CUPS | 28 OUNCES | 850 MILLILITERS

Place the milk and guava paste in a blender and blend to completely break down the guava paste and mix it thoroughly with the milk, about 1 1/2 minutes. Add the crème fraîche and ice cream and pulse several times to begin breaking up the ice cream. With the blender motor off, use a flexible spatula to mash the mixture down onto the blender blades. Continue pulsing, stopping, and mashing until the mixture is well blended, thick, and moves easily in the blender jar, roughly 30 to 90 seconds. Pour into a chilled glass or glasses, and serve at once.

Cream Cheese and Black Pepper Variation

Follow the recipe for the Sweet Guava and Crème Fraîche Shake, substituting 1/4 cup (about 2 ounces/57 grams) room temperature cream cheese for the crème fraîche and adding it to the blender along with the guava paste. Add 1/4 teaspoon freshly and very finely ground black pepper along with the ice cream.

Tamarind Shake with Sugar and Chile

Have you ever wondered what ingredient was responsible for that distinctly fresh, bright, fruity flavor in a really great plate of pad thai? The answer is tamarind, a fruit that figures prominently in Southeast Asian, Indian, and Latin American cooking. "A shake inspired by pad thai?" you may ask yourself. Indeed, and it could only have come from the inventive (which is a nice euphemism for slightly deranged) mind of my friend Dawn (who, by the way, developed an incredible pad thai recipe when we worked together at *Cook's Illustrated*).

The fruit grows as a very tart pulp inside a seedpod. In Asian, Indian, and Latin American markets (or at www.grocerythai.com or www.templeofthai.com) you may find whole dried pods, jamlike or liquid concentrates, or a compressed block of pulp (with or without seeds), which is the type I use here because of its vivid tangy flavor.

The sugar and chile, and the salt in the variation that follows, further mimic the flavors of pad thai.

5 ounces (about 142 grams) tamarind pulp, cut into several chunks

3/4 cup water (about 6 ounces/180 milliliters)

2 tablespoons sugar (about 1 ounce/24 grams)

1/4 teaspoon cayenne pepper, or to taste

8 medium scoops French vanilla ice cream (about 1 quart/24 ounces/ 680 grams), softened until just melty at the edges

For the tamarind puree Place the tamarind and water in a small saucepan over medium heat and bring to a simmer, stirring and mashing the tamarind with a wooden spoon, about 4 minutes. Off the heat, steep the tamarind pulp in water until completely softened, about 20 minutes. Strain the mixture into a small bowl, pressing on the solids to release as much puree as possible. Cover and keep at room temperature until ready to use (or up to 3 days).

For the shake Place 6 tablespoons of the tamarind puree, sugar, cayenne, and ice cream in a blender and pulse several times to begin breaking up the ice cream. With the blender motor off, use a flexible spatula to mash the mixture down onto the blender blades. Continue pulsing, stopping, and mashing until the mixture is well blended, thick, and moves easily in the blender jar, roughly 30 to 90 seconds. Pour into a chilled glass or glasses, and serve at once.

Salted Variation

Follow the recipe for the Tamarind Shake, adding a small pinch of salt to the blender with the tamarind puree, sugar, cayenne, and ice cream.

Peach Shake with Brandy and Nutmeg

Just as the late Ella Fitzgerald was known as the First Lady of Song, the late Edna Lewis could easily have been called the First Lady of Flavor. Her appreciation for great local ingredients, pitch-perfect sense of taste, and deep knowledge of southern cooking and food-ways shone bright in her books. My sister Amanda turned me on to the recipe for an unusual brandy and nutmeg dessert sauce in *The Gift of Southern Cooking*, Miss Lewis's last book, co-written with Scott Peacock (Knopf, 2003). The recipe headnote suggests serving the sauce with peach cobbler, a combination that seemed perfect for a milkshake. A dusting of the grated nutmeg is a natural garnish here.

MAKES ABOUT 3 1/2 CUPS | 28 OUNCES | 850 MILLILITERS

¼ cup cold whole or lowfat milk (about 2 ounces/60 milliliters)

⅓ cup cognac or brandy (about 2 ½ ounces/ 75 milliliters)

1 ½ tablespoons peach jam or preserves (about ¾ ounce/21 grams)

½ teaspoon pure vanilla extract

½ teaspoon freshly grated nutmeg, plus extra for garnish, if desired

4 medium scoops peach ice cream (about 1 pint/12 ounces/ 340 grams), softened until just melty at the edges

4 medium scoops peach sorbet (about 1 pint/12 ounces/ 340 grams), softened until just melty at the edges

Place the milk, cognac, jam, vanilla extract, and nutmeg in a blender and blend to mix thoroughly, about 15 seconds. Add the ice cream and sorbet and pulse several times to begin breaking them up. With the blender motor off, use a flexible spatula to mash the mixture down onto the blender blades. Continue pulsing, stopping, and mashing until the mixture is well blended, thick, and moves easily in the blender jar, roughly 30 to 90 seconds. Pour into a chilled glass or glasses, and serve at once.

Facing page: Peach Shake with Brandy and Nutmeg.

Tomato-Peach Shake

The combination of tomatoes and peaches surprises some people, but they shouldn't wag their fingers before trying it. The sweetness of the peach ice cream and sorbet brings out the delicate acidity in great, ripe, red tomatoes to create a high summer synergy in the glass. And the color! The tomato gives this shake the same coral color as some of the most spectacular sunsets I've seen.

Note the mention of high summer. Don't bother with off-season supermarket or packaged tomatoes. This shake is really meant for peak-season, perfectly ripe, local fruit from a farmers' market (or your own backyard, if you can swing that).

2 medium, ripe, local tomatoes (about 12 ounces/ 340 grams), cored, halved, and seeded

Pinch of ground cinnamon

6 medium scoops peach ice cream (about 1 1/2 pints/ 18 ounces/510 grams), softened until just melty at the edges

2 medium scoops peach sorbet (about 1/2 pint/6 ounces/ 170 grams), softened until just melty at the edges

MAKES ABOUT 3 1/2 CUPS | 28 OUNCES | 850 MILLILITERS

Grate the tomato halves on the large holes of a box grater (with the cut sides of the halves on the grating plane) until the pulp has been grated and only the skins remain (you will have about 1 1/2 cups/9 ounces/255 grams pulp); discard the skins. Place the tomato pulp, cinnamon, ice cream, and sorbet in a blender and pulse several times to begin breaking up the ice cream and sorbet. With the blender motor off, use a flexible spatula to mash the mixture down onto the blender blades. Continue pulsing, stopping, and mashing until the mixture is well blended, thick, and moves easily in the blender jar, roughly 30 to 90 seconds. Pour into a chilled glass or glasses, and serve at once.

White Peach Melba Shake with Raspberry Granita

White peaches are less acidic than their yellow counterparts, and as a result their sweet flavor is much more delicate. You know what's coming next . . . make this shake *only when you have perfectly ripe, fragrant, local white peaches* at the height of their season. Otherwise, you'll wonder, "What's the big whoop?"

The raspberry granita is lighter and icier than many others, and that is by design. I wanted to adjust the flavor to complement the white peaches without overwhelming them. By the way, the granita makes a great topping for the *Serious* Chocolate Shake (page 44), too.

(Recipe on next page)

¼ cup sugar (about
2 ounces/48 grams)

¾ cup water (about
6 ounces/180 milliliters)

Pinch of salt

¾ cup fresh or
frozen (and thawed)
raspberries (about
3 ounces/85 grams)

2 large, ripe, super
fragrant white peaches
(about 12 ounces/
340 grams), pitted,
peeled, and cut
into chunks

⅛ teaspoon freshly
squeezed lemon juice

3 medium scoops
vanilla bean or original
vanilla ice cream (about
¾ pint/9 ounces/
255 grams), softened
until just melty
at the edges

3 medium scoops
peach sorbet (about
¾ pint/9 ounces/
255 grams), softened
until just melty
at the edges

For the granita Bring the sugar and water to a gentle boil in a small saucepan over medium-high heat, swirling the pan to dissolve the sugar; reduce the heat to medium and simmer for 3 minutes. Off the heat, cool the syrup to room temperature. Place the syrup, salt, and raspberries in a blender and puree until smooth. Strain the raspberry mixture (pressing on the solids to extract as much puree as possible) into a shallow container. Cover and freeze until softly frozen (not solid), $2\frac{1}{2}$ to 3 hours. Remove from the freezer and gently run a dinner fork through the frozen mass to break it down into loose, icy crystals. Cover the container and return it to the freezer. Freeze until firm, checking and raking the granita with the fork every hour or two to keep the crystals loose and fine, at least 7 hours.

For the shake Place the peach chunks and lemon juice in a blender and blend to break down the peaches completely, about 1 minute. Add the ice cream and sorbet and pulse several times to begin breaking them up. With the blender motor off, use a flexible spatula to mash the mixture down onto the blender blades. Continue pulsing, stopping, and mashing until the mixture is well blended, thick, and moves easily in the blender jar, roughly 30 to 90 seconds. Pour into a chilled glass or glasses, top each with $\frac{1}{2}$ cup ($2\frac{1}{2}$ ounces/70 grams) granita, and serve at once.

Apricot-Amaretto Shake

There are several kinds of almond-flavored liqueur, but the archetype is Disaronno Originale, made in Saronno in the Lombardy region of Italy, and sold in dimpled rectangular bottles with blocklike square caps. Amaretto, as the liqueur is popularly known, certainly has a distinct almond flavor, but the nuts themselves may or may not be part of its formulation. Many sources, including the company's own Web site, credit the drink's almond flavor to the oil from apricot kernels, the almond-shaped nubbins inside the apricot pits. No wonder apricots and amaretto have such a strong affinity.

Briefly cooking fresh apricots into a simple sauce both assures that they blend thoroughly into the shake, and provides a brighter fruit flavor than apricot jam, nectar, or syrup. Don't bother peeling the apricots; their thin skins break down and are unnoticeable in the shake.

Amaretti biscotti, which are small, round, Italian almond cookies, would make a great garnish. Packed in a bright red, square tin, Lazzaroni Amaretti di Saronno is a popular brand, available at Italian markets or online at www.doma-italian-market.com or www.ditalia.com.

(Recipe on next page)

5 medium, ripe apricots (about 8 ounces/ 227 grams), pitted and cut into eighths

3 tablespoons sugar (about 1 1/2 ounces/36 grams)

3 tablespoons amaretto liqueur (about 1 1/2 ounces/ 45 milliliters)

1/2 teaspoon pure almond extract

8 medium scoops vanilla bean or original vanilla ice cream (about 1 quart/24 ounces/ 680 grams), softened until just melty at the edges

For the apricots Stir the apricots and sugar together in a small saucepan over medium heat, cover, and cook until the apricots release their juices, about 4 minutes. Remove the cover, reduce the heat to low, and simmer, stirring occasionally, until the apricots break down, about 6 minutes longer. Off the heat, cool the mixture to room temperature, then cover and refrigerate for at least 30 minutes (or up to 3 days).

For the shake Place 6 tablespoons of the apricot mixture, amaretto, and almond extract in a blender and blend until smooth, about 30 seconds. Add the ice cream and pulse several times to begin breaking it up. With the blender motor off, use a flexible spatula to mash the mixture down onto the blender blades. Continue pulsing, stopping, and mashing until the mixture is well blended, thick, and moves easily in the blender jar, roughly 30 to 90 seconds. Pour into a chilled glass or glasses, and serve at once.

Poire William Shake

Determined as I was to avoid calling for specific flavors of particular ice cream brands for these shakes, there was no way to ignore Häagen-Dazs Caramelized Pear and Toasted Pecan ice cream. It is simply too delicious to pass by. Happily, it was the perfect partner for my favorite *digestif*, Poire William, a pear-flavored *eau de vie*, the French term for a clear, strong, fruit brandy.

France is an important producer of *eaux de vie*, especially in the Alsace region, but similar spirits are made elsewhere as well, notably in Germany, the Czech Republic, Slovakia, Poland, Hungary, Switzerland, and the United States—see www.clearcreekdistillery.com. A good *eau de vie*, which means "water of life," is intensely aromatic with the essence of the fresh fruit. With absolutely no hint of sweetness, an *eau de vie* is usually served after the meal, to aid digestion.

While living in France I developed a keen appreciation for Poire William that was nurtured by the owner of our neighborhood *cave*, or wine shop. My French was lousy and so was her English, so she taught me through tasting more than discussion, which made for quite a few very happy afternoons.

If you can't find Häagen-Dazs Caramelized Pear and Toasted Pecan ice cream, substitute pear sorbet. The result will be less nuanced, but more pear-forward.

(Recipe on next page)

2 teaspoons unsalted
butter (about
1/3 ounce/8 grams)

1 medium, ripe Bartlett
or Comice pear (about
8 ounces/227 grams),
peeled, cored and
roughly chopped

6 tablespoons cold
whole or lowfat milk
(about 3 ounces/
90 milliliters)

2 1/2 tablespoons Poire
William (about
1 1/4 ounces/
40 milliliters)

4 medium scoops
Häagen-Dazs
Caramelized Pear and
Toasted Pecan ice
cream (about 1 pint/
12 ounces/340 grams),
softened until just
melty at the edges

4 medium scoops
French vanilla ice
cream (about 1 pint/
12 ounces/340 grams),
softened until just
melty at the edges

MAKES ABOUT 3 1/2 CUPS | 28 OUNCES | 850 MILLILITERS

Melt the butter in a medium nonstick skillet over medium heat and heat until it stops foaming. Add the pear and cook, stirring occasionally, until soft and translucent, about 4 minutes. Off the heat, cool the pear to room temperature, about 15 minutes. Place the cooled pear, milk, and Poire William in a blender and blend to mix thoroughly, about 30 seconds. Add the ice cream and pulse several times to begin breaking it up. With the blender motor off, use a flexible spatula to mash the mixture down onto the blender blades. Continue pulsing, stopping, and mashing until the mixture is well blended, thick, and moves easily in the blender jar, roughly 30 to 90 seconds. Pour into a chilled glass or glasses, and serve at once.

Minted Cucumber–Lemon Shake

This shake renewed my respect for cucumbers. They are, inarguably, cool, crunchy, and at home in any number of salads, but I've always found their flavor to be fleeting, so I wasn't certain they'd have enough oomph for a milkshake. The trusty cukes proved me wrong, though—their ethereal flavor came through loud and clear. If you can get your hands on some fresh peppermint, try it. It's even spicier than the usual spearmint.

¼ cup cold whole or lowfat milk (about 2 ounces/60 milliliters)

1 medium cucumber (about 10 ounces/ 284 grams), peeled, seeded, and cut into chunks

1 tablespoon minced fresh mint

4 medium scoops vanilla bean or original vanilla ice cream (about 1 pint/12 ounces/ 340 grams), softened until just melty at the edges

4 medium scoops lemon sorbet (about 1 pint/12 ounces/ 340 grams), softened until just melty at the edges

MAKES ABOUT 3½ CUPS | 28 OUNCES | 850 MILLILITERS

Place the milk, cucumber, and mint in a blender and blend to break down the cucumber completely, about 1 minute. Add the ice cream and sorbet and pulse several times to begin breaking them up. With the blender motor off, use a flexible spatula to mash the mixture down onto the blender blades. Continue pulsing, stopping, and mashing until the mixture is well blended, thick, and moves easily in the blender jar, roughly 30 to 90 seconds. Pour into a chilled glass or glasses, and serve at once.

Honeydew-Cucumber Shake with Cucumber Granita

So pale is this shake's green shade that you could almost call it silver. A cap of luminous, icy, cucumber-flavored granita, even paler green if that's possible, completes a look that is about as debonair as a milkshake can be. The high water content of honeydew gives this shake a slightly thinner and even more slurpable consistency than most of the others. Use any type of cucumber you wish for the granita.

(Recipe on next page)

*Facing page: Honeydew-Cucumber Shake
with Cucumber Granita.*

2 tablespoons
sugar (about
1 ounce/24 grams)

2 tablespoons water
(about 1 ounce/
30 milliliters)

Pinch of salt

1 tablespoon freshly
squeezed lime juice

3/4 medium cucumber
(about 8 ounces/
227 grams), peeled,
seeded, and roughly
chopped (about 1 cup)

1/2 small, ripe
honeydew melon
(about 1 pound/
454 grams), peeled,
seeded, and cut into
1 1/2-inch (4 centimeter)
chunks (about 3 cups)

6 medium scoops
vanilla bean or original
vanilla ice cream
(about 1 1/2 pints/
18 ounces/510 grams),
softened until just
melty at the edges

For the granita Bring the sugar and water to a gentle boil in a small saucepan over medium-high heat, swirling the pan to dissolve the sugar; reduce the heat to medium and simmer for 2 minutes. Off the heat, cool the syrup to room temperature. Place the syrup, salt, 2 teaspoons of the lime juice, and the cucumber in a blender and puree until smooth. Pour the cucumber mixture into a shallow container. Cover and freeze until softly frozen (not solid), 2 1/2 to 3 hours. Remove from the freezer and gently run a dinner fork through the frozen mass to break it down into loose, icy crystals. Cover the container and return it to the freezer. Freeze until firm, checking and raking the granita with the fork every hour or two to keep the crystals loose and fine, at least 7 hours.

For the shake Place 1/2 cup (about 2 1/2 ounces/ 70 grams) of granita, the honeydew, and the remaining 1 teaspoon of lime juice in a blender and blend to break down the honeydew completely, about 1 minute. Add the ice cream and pulse several times to begin breaking it up. With the blender motor off, use a flexible spatula to mash the mixture down onto the blender blades. Continue pulsing, stopping, and mashing until the mixture is well blended, thick, and moves easily in the blender jar, roughly 30 to 90 seconds. Pour into a chilled glass or glasses, top each with 1/2 cup (about 2 1/2 ounces/70 grams) granita, and serve at once.

Prune-Armagnac Shake

Armagnac, the brandy from the Gascony region in southwestern France, may not be as well known as its more famous cousin, cognac, but it is certainly no second fiddle. Arguably, Armagnac tastes even richer and earthier than cognac. It's usually drunk as a *digestif* after the meal, but it also pairs well with certain sweets, among them prunes, another product of the region. The combination shows up in cakes, tarts, custards, and ice cream (and as a classic accompaniment to foie gras), and of course, in milkshakes. At least in this book.

Armagnac and prunes are very distinctive flavors on their own, but I didn't stop there with the combination. I mingled it with the common French practice of softening prunes in tea (often as a nonalcoholic alternative to Armagnac) before baking with them. The tea is wonderful, adding both depth and a flavorful backbone that highlights the prunes and Armagnac even further.

8 or 9 small pitted prunes (about 2 ounces/57 grams), quartered

6 tablespoons strong black tea, hot or room temperature (about 3 ounces/90 milliliters)

¼ cup Armagnac (2 ounces/60 milliliters)

¼ teaspoon pure vanilla extract

7 medium scoops French vanilla ice cream (about 1 ¾ pints/21 ounces/ 595 grams), softened until just melty at the edges

MAKES ABOUT 3½ CUPS | 28 OUNCES | 850 MILLILITERS

Place the prunes and tea in a small bowl and set aside to soak for 1 hour. Place the soaked prunes, the tea used to soak them, Armagnac, and vanilla extract in a blender and blend to break down the prunes completely, about 45 seconds. Add the ice cream and pulse several times to begin breaking it up. With the blender motor off, use a flexible spatula to mash the mixture down onto the blender blades. Continue pulsing, stopping, and mashing until the mixture is well blended, thick, and moves easily in the blender jar, roughly 30 to 90 seconds. Pour into a chilled glass or glasses, and serve at once.

Prune-Armagnac with Chocolate Variation

Follow the recipe for the Prune-Armagnac Shake, substituting 1 scoop (¼ pint/3 ounces/85 grams) of chocolate sorbet for 1 scoop (¼ pint/3 ounces/85 grams) of the vanilla ice cream.

Cantaloupe-Lemon Shake

One of the dogs my family had when I was a kid, a fiery wheaten terrier named Tober, was a cantaloupe fiend. He loved the stuff, and would even catch chunks you threw for him in midair. I'm as enthusiastic as Tober was, though less likely to leap for my 'loupe. Tober might not have gone for the lemon here—I think it accentuates the melon's sweetness—but this is his shake nonetheless. Like in the Honeydew-Cucumber Shake (page 131), the melon gives this shake a loose consistency.

½ medium, ripe cantaloupe (about 1 pound/454 grams), peeled, seeded, and cut into 1½-inch (4 centimeter) chunks (about 3 cups)

¼ teaspoon freshly squeezed lemon juice

3 medium scoops vanilla bean or original vanilla ice cream (about ¾ pint/9 ounces/ 255 grams), softened until just melty at the edges

3 medium scoops lemon sorbet (about ¾ pint/9 ounces/ 255 grams), softened until just melty at the edges

MAKES ABOUT 3½ CUPS | 28 OUNCES | 850 MILLILITERS

Place the cantaloupe and lemon juice in a blender and blend to break down the cantaloupe completely, about 1 minute. Add the ice cream and sorbet and pulse several times to begin breaking them up. With the blender motor off, use a flexible spatula to mash the mixture down onto the blender blades. Continue pulsing, stopping, and mashing until the mixture is well blended, thick, and moves easily in the blender jar, roughly 30 to 90 seconds. Pour into a chilled glass or glasses, and serve at once.

Facing page: Watermelon Agua Fresca (foreground, page 188) and Cantaloupe-Lemon Shake.

Lemon-Thyme Shake

Many people consider mint to be *the* dessert herb, but it is just the tip of the herbal iceberg. Other fresh herbs, such as basil, rosemary, or thyme can give sweets an unexpected, aromatic twist that leaves people tasting and thinking and tasting and thinking, trying to identify that extra something special in the flavor.

That's just what the thyme does here; it adds a woodsy, elegant yet familiar note that really takes this otherwise mild lemon shake to a higher level.

5 tablespoons sugar (about 2 ½ ounces/60 grams)

Zest of 1 medium lemon, removed in strips using a vegetable peeler

⅔ cup water (about 5 ounces/150 milliliters)

2 tablespoons plus 1 teaspoon minced fresh thyme

6 medium scoops vanilla bean or original vanilla ice cream (about 1 ½ pints/ 18 ounces/510 grams), softened until just melty at the edges

2 medium scoops lemon sorbet (about ½ pint/6 ounces/ 170 grams), softened until just melty at the edges

MAKES ABOUT 3 ½ CUPS | 28 OUNCES | 850 MILLILITERS

For the lemon-thyme syrup Place the sugar and lemon zest in a small saucepan and stir them together until the sugar is moist and fragrant. Add the water, set the pan over medium-high heat, and bring to a gentle boil, swirling the pan to dissolve the sugar. Reduce the heat to medium and simmer for 3 minutes. Off the heat, add 2 tablespoons of the thyme, swirl the pan to distribute, and cool the syrup to room temperature. Cover the pan and set aside to steep overnight (or at least 4 hours). Strain the syrup into a small bowl, pressing on the lemon zest and thyme to release all the liquid, cover, and refrigerate for at least 30 minutes (or up to 5 days).

For the shake Place ½ cup (about 4 ounces/125 milliliters) of the chilled lemon-thyme syrup and remaining 1 teaspoon minced thyme in a blender and blend to mix thoroughly, about 30 seconds. Add the ice cream and sorbet and pulse several times to begin breaking them up. With the blender motor off, use a flexible spatula to mash the mixture down onto the blender blades. Continue pulsing, stopping, and mashing until the mixture is well blended, thick, and moves easily in the blender jar, roughly 30 to 90 seconds. Pour into a chilled glass or glasses, and serve at once.

Lemon-Buttermilk Shake

Lemon and buttermilk are both tangy, and you might think that two tangs would be overkill. But then the vanilla ice cream works its sweet magic, pulling the whole concoction into a gentle, intriguing balance. Most supermarkets carry lowfat and/or nonfat buttermilk. I think the latter has a chalky aftertaste, so if you're not using whole, the better option of the two is the lowfat buttermilk. A few fresh raspberries or blueberries, or sliced strawberries, or a thin slice of fresh lemon make a lovely garnish.

½ cup cold whole or lowfat buttermilk (about 4 ounces/ 125 milliliters)

1 tablespoon honey (about ¾ ounce/22 grams)

4 medium scoops vanilla bean or original vanilla ice cream (about 1 pint/12 ounces/ 340 grams), softened until just melty at the edges

4 medium scoops lemon sorbet (about 1 pint/12 ounces/ 340 grams), softened until just melty at the edges

MAKES ABOUT 3½ CUPS | 28 OUNCES | 850 MILLILITERS

Place the buttermilk and honey in a blender and blend to mix thoroughly, about 15 seconds. Add the ice cream and sorbet and pulse several times to begin breaking them up. With the blender motor off, use a flexible spatula to mash the mixture down onto the blender blades. Continue pulsing, stopping, and mashing until the mixture is well blended, thick, and moves easily in the blender jar, roughly 30 to 90 seconds. Pour into a chilled glass or glasses, and serve at once.

Facing page: Lemon-Buttermilk Shake.

Date-Buttermilk Shake

Throughout the desert landscape of southeastern California, in the Coachella and Bard valleys, fresh dates grow in impressive clusters that dangle from regal date palms. Most of the dates are dried, which concentrates their already high sugar content, about 55 percent, so they become super sweet and almost fudgy in texture.

Because dates themselves are so sweet, the date shakes that are a regional specialty at date gardens, ice cream parlors, and burger joints all through the area tend to be awfully sweet as well. In this interpretation of the classic, I tame the sweetness with a little something tart—buttermilk.

Deglet Noor and Medjool are two of the most common date varieties, and both work beautifully in the shakes. Dates should be available at supermarkets, but in case you need an online source, try www.shieldsdates.com, or www.oasisdategardens.com. A sprinkle of freshly grated nutmeg is a traditional date shake garnish.

8 medium dried dates (about 4 1/2 ounces/ 128 grams), pitted and roughly chopped (a scant 1/2 cup)

1/2 cup cold whole or lowfat buttermilk (about 4 ounces/ 125 milliliters)

1/4 teaspoon pure vanilla extract

7 medium scoops French vanilla ice cream (about 1 3/4 pints/21 ounces/ 595 grams), softened until just melty at the edges

MAKES ABOUT 3 1/2 CUPS | 28 OUNCES | 850 MILLILITERS

To soften the dates Place the dates and water to cover in a small saucepan set over medium-high heat and bring to a simmer. Off the heat, cool the mixture to room temperature, then drain the dates.

For the shake Place the buttermilk, vanilla extract, and dates in a blender and blend to break down the dates completely, about 1 minute. Add the ice cream and pulse several times to begin breaking it up. With the blender motor off, use a flexible spatula to mash the mixture down onto the blender blades. Continue pulsing, stopping, and mashing until the mixture is well blended, thick, and moves easily in the blender jar, roughly 30 to 90 seconds. Pour into a chilled glass or glasses, and serve at once.

Date-Buttermilk with Brandy and Nutmeg Variation

Follow the recipe for the Date-Buttermilk Shake, adding 3 tablespoons of brandy or cognac (about 1½ ounces/45 milliliters) and a pinch of freshly grated nutmeg to the blender with the other ingredients.

Date-Buttermilk with Ginger Variation

Follow the recipe for the Date-Buttermilk Shake, substituting 2 teaspoons of grated fresh ginger for the vanilla extract and 4 scoops (about 1 pint/12 ounces/340 grams) of ginger ice cream for 4 scoops (about 1 pint/12 ounces/ 340 grams) of the vanilla ice cream.

Sgroppino al Limone

Though it's not technically a shake, this cool, lemony cocktail from the Veneto region of Italy, also the home of Prosecco, does include lemon sorbet, which puts it in the ballpark at least. As the sugar cube dissolves, it provides a bit of sweetness to balance the tart lemon and the strong vodka. Serve in champagne flutes before dinner, as a palate cleanser between courses, or after the meal to accompany, follow, or even *be* dessert.

2 tablespoons
vodka (1 ounce)

1 ½ scoops lemon
sorbet (about ⅓ pint/
4 ½ ounces/128 grams)

Chilled Prosecco
or other sparkling
white wine

2 sugar cubes

2 lemon twists

MAKES 2

Whisk the vodka and 1 scoop (½ cup/3 ounces/86 grams) sorbet together in a small bowl until the texture is uniform. Add enough sparkling wine to fill each of two flutes about three-quarters full and whisk gently to combine.

Place one sugar cube in each flute, divide the sorbet mixture between the two flutes, and top each with half of the remaining ½ scoop (¼ cup/1 ½ ounces/42 grams) sorbet. Run a lemon peel around the rim of each flute, twist it over the top, then drop it into the flute and serve at once.

Facing page: Sgroppino al Limone.

Sour Cherry and Sour Cream Shake

Cold sour cherry soup is a standard Hungarian summer dish. Called *meggyleves*, the soup has been around for eons and has therefore morphed into a thousand different versions, but one classic is flavored with cinnamon and enriched with either (or both) fresh cream or a tart, cultured cream such as crème fraîche or sour cream. Seems like a natural starting point for a shake, if you ask me.

The adjective "sour" refers less to the nature of the soup and more to the kind of cherries from which it's made. Sour cherries are bright red, small, and generally pretty soft, a totally different beast from the sweet, big, beefy, burgundy beauties we eat out of hand every summer.

The most common sour cherry varieties in the United States are Morello and Montmorency, but we rarely see them fresh because there is little demand. (I, lucky one that I was, had a steady summer supply because there was a sour cherry tree in my backyard until last winter, when it broke in two from the weight of accumulated ice and snow. Drat!) So we buy them either in jars, usually packed in a very light syrup, or frozen. If you have a choice, buy a jar so you can strain the syrup to use in the shake (jars are available online at www.kalustyans.com). If frozen sour cherries are your only option, buy a bottle of cherry juice, too.

6 tablespoons sour cherries, chopped (about 3 ounces/85 grams)

6 tablespoons light cherry syrup (from the jar of cherries) or cherry juice (about 3 ounces/90 milliliters)

3 tablespoons sour cream (about 2 1/2 ounces/70 grams)

1 tablespoon light brown sugar (about 1/2 ounce/12 grams)

1/4 teaspoon pure vanilla extract

1/4 teaspoon ground cinnamon

7 medium scoops original vanilla or vanilla bean ice cream (about 1 3/4 pints/ 21 ounces/595 grams), softened until just melty at the edges

MAKES ABOUT 3 1/2 CUPS | 28 OUNCES | 850 MILLILITERS

If using sour cherries from a jar, strain the syrup but don't discard. Place the sour cherries, cherry syrup or juice, sour cream, brown sugar, vanilla extract, and cinnamon in a blender and blend to break down the cherries completely, about 30 seconds. Add the ice cream and pulse several times to begin breaking it up. With the blender motor off, use a flexible spatula to mash the mixture down onto the blender blades. Continue pulsing, stopping, and mashing until the mixture is well blended, thick, and moves easily in the blender jar, roughly 30 to 90 seconds. Pour into a chilled glass or glasses, and serve at once.

UNCONVENTIONAL SHAKES

Sweet Corn and Basil Shake

If you have ever grated an ear of fresh corn to make corn chowder or griddle cakes, you know that this vegetable is surprisingly creamy. And of course, fresh, local sweet corn is one of summer's most sublime taste treats. So why not combine corn's natural taste and textural talents into an uncommon shake? Basil, another hallmark hot weather flavor, adds extra dimension and summer ambience.

It goes without saying that local corn is best. Choose a yellow variety to give the shake a gorgeous golden hue.

6 tablespoons sugar (about 3 ounces/72 grams)

2/3 cup dry white wine (about 5 ounces/ 150 milliliters)

1 cup packed fresh basil leaves, roughly chopped (about 2 ounces/57 grams)

2 medium ears of local yellow corn, husks and silks removed (about 20 ounces/567 grams)

3 tablespoons water (about 1 1/2 ounces/ 45 milliliters)

8 medium scoops vanilla bean or original vanilla ice cream (about 1 quart/24 ounces/ 680 grams), softened until just melty at the edges

MAKES ABOUT 3 1/2 CUPS | 28 OUNCES | 850 MILLILITERS

For the basil syrup and corn Mix the sugar and wine in a small saucepan over medium heat, swirling the pan occasionally to dissolve the sugar. Bring the mixture to a gentle boil, reduce the heat to medium-low, and simmer for 3 minutes. Off the heat, add the chopped basil, and stir to immerse it in the liquid. Cover the pan and set aside to steep for 1 hour. Strain the syrup into a small bowl, pressing on the basil to release all the liquid, cover, and refrigerate for at least 30 minutes (or up to 3 days).

Break the ears of corn in half. Working with half an ear at a time, stand the broken end on a cutting board and, using a chef's knife, cut the kernels off the cob a few rows at a time, placing the cut kernels into a small saucepan or skillet as you go (you should have about 2 cups/10 ounces/284 grams). Place the pan over medium heat, add the water, cover the pan, and simmer until the corn kernels are tender and bright yellow, about 5 minutes. Off the heat, cool the corn to room temperature, about 15 minutes.

For the shake Place 6 tablespoons (3 ounces/ 90 milliliters) of the chilled basil syrup and the corn in a blender and blend to break down the corn completely and mix thoroughly, about 1 minute. Add the ice cream and pulse several times to begin breaking it up. With the blender motor off, use a flexible spatula to mash the mixture down onto the blender blades. Continue pulsing, stopping, and mashing until the mixture is well blended, thick, and moves easily in the blender jar, roughly 30 to 90 seconds. Pour into a chilled glass or glasses, and serve at once.

Mexican Street Vendor Corn with Chile and Lime Variation

Follow the recipe for the Sweet Corn and Basil Shake, omitting the basil syrup and adding $1/4$ cup freshly squeezed lime juice (about 2 ounces/60 milliliters), 4 teaspoons crème fraîche (about 1 ounce/28 grams), $1 1/2$ teaspoons pure chile powder (preferably New Mexico), and a pinch of cayenne to the blender with the corn kernels.

Spiced Pumpkin Shake

Canned pumpkin puree is a beautiful color, and it certainly contributes to this shake's gorgeous, muted orange hue and extra thick, velvety texture. No matter how much puree I added, though, I still wanted a stronger pumpkin flavor.

My sister Amanda, the queen of all things autumnal, knew exactly what to do—break out the pumpkin butter (she had a cupboard full of it, mostly homemade!). With tons of squashy flavor and a marked sweetness, the pumpkin butter gave this shake exactly the boost it needed to achieve greatness. Of course we also tried store-bought pumpkin butter, and found that flavor varies substantially from brand to brand; Stonewall Kitchen's Maple Pumpkin Butter was our favorite (www.stonewallkitchen.com).

6 tablespoons cold whole or lowfat milk (about 3 ounces/ 90 milliliters)

3 tablespoons pumpkin butter (about 1 1/2 ounces/43 grams)

2/3 cup canned pumpkin puree (about 5 ounces/142 grams)

1/2 teaspoon ground cinnamon

Pinch of ground cloves

Pinch of freshly grated nutmeg

8 medium scoops French vanilla ice cream (about 1 quart/24 ounces/ 680 grams), softened until just melty at the edges

MAKES ABOUT 3 1/2 CUPS | 28 OUNCES | 850 MILLILITERS

Place the milk, pumpkin butter and puree, cinnamon, cloves, and nutmeg in a blender and blend to mix thoroughly, about 30 seconds. Add the ice cream and pulse several times to begin breaking it up. With the blender motor off, use a flexible spatula to mash the mixture down onto the blender blades. Continue pulsing, stopping, and mashing until the mixture is well blended, thick, and moves easily in the blender jar, roughly 30 to 90 seconds. Pour into a chilled glass or glasses, and serve at once.

Spiced Pumpkin with Bourbon Variation

Follow the recipe for the Spiced Pumpkin Shake, adding 3 tablespoons of bourbon (about 1 1/2 ounces/45 milliliters) to the blender with the milk, pumpkin butter and puree, cinnamon, cloves, and nutmeg.

Facing page: Spiced Pumpkin (background) and Tarte Tatin (foreground, page 163) shakes.

Zabaglione Shake

Maybe neither culture would like to admit it, but Italian and French cooking sometimes mirror each other. Think of hunter's-style chicken, *cacciatore* to the Italians and *chasseur* to the French. The concept is the same—poultry (as the name indicates, in the mists of time it was probably whatever bird was bagged during the day's hunt) braised with mushrooms, tomatoes, wine, and whatever other ingredients the locale offers.

Among desserts, Italian zabaglione and French sabayon are almost identical sweet, aerated, wine-flavored egg custards, sometimes served on their own and sometimes as a sauce for another dessert dish.

Sweet marsala is the classic flavoring in zabaglione, though you could also use Madeira or amontillado sherry. Sliced strawberries are a traditional accompaniment, hence the strawberry variation.

2 tablespoons sugar (about 1 ounce/24 grams)

2 teaspoons finely grated lemon zest

1/2 cup sweet marsala, Madeira, or amontillado sherry (about 4 ounces/ 125 milliliters)

1 teaspoon pure vanilla extract

8 medium scoops French vanilla ice cream (about 1 quart/24 ounces/ 680 grams), softened until just melty at the edges

MAKES ABOUT 3 1/2 CUPS | 28 OUNCES | 850 MILLILITERS

Place the sugar and lemon zest in a small bowl and stir them together until the sugar is moist and fragrant. Place the Marsala, vanilla extract, and lemon sugar in a blender and blend to mix thoroughly, about 15 seconds. Add the ice cream and pulse several times to begin breaking it up. With the blender motor off, use a flexible spatula to mash the mixture down onto the blender blades. Continue pulsing, stopping, and mashing until the mixture is well blended, thick, and moves easily in the blender jar, roughly 30 to 90 seconds. Pour into a chilled glass or glasses, and serve at once.

Zabaglione with Strawberries Variation

Follow the recipe for the Zabaglione Shake, substituting 3 scoops (³/₄ pint/9 ounces/255 grams) of strawberry sorbet for 3 scoops (³/₄ pint/9 ounces/255 grams) of the vanilla ice cream.

Laura's Rapture—
Raspberry-Chocolate Concrete

This is a version of the Ted Drewes concrete that makes Laura swoon (see The Cult of the Concrete, page 154). She opted for vanilla custard, raspberries, and chocolate chips. I replace the chips with fudge sauce, which accentuates the lush texture of the custard.

Personally, I could swing either direction with the custard flavor. Laura says the classic choice is vanilla, and it certainly makes a terrific background for the sweet-tart berries. Since I subscribe to the "more chocolate is better" theory, I couldn't resist trying the concrete with chocolate custard, too. The berries work beautifully here, as well—I think this chocolate double-hitter is a winner.

Choose a high-quality chocolate sauce such as Fran's from Seattle (available online at www.franschocolates.com). It will be thicker and more deeply flavored than most supermarket offerings.

2 cups vanilla or chocolate frozen custard (about 16 ounces/454 grams)

2/3 cup fresh or thawed frozen raspberries (about 5 ounces/142 grams)

2 teaspoons sugar (about 1 ounce/24 grams)

1/2 cup high-quality chocolate or fudge sauce, at room temperature (about 4 ounces/125 milliliters)

MAKES ABOUT 2 1/2 CUPS | 20 OUNCES | 600 MILLILITERS

Remove the frozen custard from the freezer and allow it to rest at room temperature until the custard at the edges of the container just begins to look melty, 10 to 15 minutes. Meanwhile, mix the raspberries and sugar in a small bowl and set aside.

Scoop the custard into another bowl, add the raspberries, and mix with a wooden spoon or spatula until the berries are largely crushed and well incorporated. Drop blobs of the chocolate sauce over the custard-raspberry mixture and mix until there are streaks and small pockets of sauce in the custard. Scoop into two chilled bowls or cups, and serve at once.

The Cult of the Concrete

Everyone knows what concrete is. It's a building material, right? Sidewalks are made of it.

Well, ask someone from St. Louis about concrete, and you'll probably get a very different answer. There, concretes are servings of super thick, super dense frozen custard, studded with any number of mix-ins in the form of candy, cookies, cake, fruit, nuts, syrup, and more. No liquid, just custard and mix-ins, so the consistency is thick enough that a spoon stuck into the center of the concrete will stay put when you hold the cup upside down. Concretes are sometimes served with a straw as well as a spoon, though I am not sure why. The straw is just not a useful tool here.

Let's start with the frozen custard. It is extra dense, rich, smooth ice cream that owes its texture to a high percentage of egg yolks and a low percentage of air incorporated as it churns. All ice cream has some air in it, which is called "overrun." The more air, the fluffier the texture; less air means a denser texture. For those who have never encountered frozen custard, the consistency is similar to soft-serve ice cream, but much, much denser.

Frozen custard is especially popular, and widely available, in the midsection of the United States. Just like ice cream, frozen custard is served in cones and sundaes, and also as shakes so thick the texture is supposed to resemble the material after which they are named, concrete.

The establishment that popularized the concrete, and with which it is still most heavily associated to this day, is Ted Drewes, on old Route 66, in St. Louis (www.teddrewes.com). My in-laws Laura and Geoff spent a few years living in St. Louis during grad school, and though they moved away years ago, the mere mention of Ted Drewes causes Laura, who is usually quite plain-spoken, to wax poetic. When I asked what she remembered about Drewes, this was her response: "Do I remember much about it?!? We speak lovingly of Ted Drewes to our children. They cannot understand why we can't just hop in the car and go get a concrete. It's just a fifteen-hour drive. To tell you the truth, I don't know either why we let that deter us. There were other places in St. Louis that served concretes, but everyone knew that the only place to get the real thing was at Ted Drewes. Please, take me back!"

So, short of moving to St. Louis, how can you sample a concrete? If you live near a frozen custard stand (visit www.custardlist.com for a state-by-state listing of them), get in the car, go there, and order one. It will be fresh, and the chances are good that you will have many mix-in options from which to choose. If a custard stand is out of your reach, you may be able to find frozen custard in some supermarkets that have deals with small local producers to sell a packaged version of their custard. If you can find some custard to bring home, try the three following recipes. Another possibility, albeit an expensive one, for obtaining frozen custard at home is to order it online. Consult www.teddrewes.com, www.newyorkstyledeli.com for Abbott's brand, or www.kopps.com. As a last resort, you can approximate the right texture with super premium ice cream. Just re-freeze it for about an hour after blending it with the mix-ins.

Incorporating the dense custard and mix-ins presents a challenge for most blenders. I tried with several different models, as well as with drink mixers, and the process was fraught with stopping, starting, scraping, tamping, and dripping. In the end, it was much simpler, and neater, to mix the old-fashioned way, with a wooden spoon and some elbow grease, in a bowl.

Chocolate-Pretzel Concrete

Accenting sweet flavors with salt is all the rage now. But the salty-sweet combo was a bold stroke in the early 1970s when my father introduced me to one of his favorite snacks, crunchy-salty-sweet chocolate-covered pretzels. In a concrete, chocolate-covered pretzels do triple duty, adding not just bursts of chocolate, but also the counterpoint of salt crystals and the hearty crunch of the pretzels.

If there are no chocolate-covered pretzels on hand, you can get away with using about 1/3 cup (about 3 ounces/85 grams) roughly crushed pretzels and 1/3 cup (about 3 ounces/85 grams) chopped semisweet or bittersweet chocolate, or even mini chocolate chips.

2 cups vanilla or chocolate frozen custard (about 16 ounces/454 grams)

6 ounces chocolate-covered pretzels (about 170 grams)

MAKES ABOUT 2 1/2 CUPS | 20 OUNCES | 600 MILLILITERS

Remove the frozen custard from the freezer and allow it to rest at room temperature until the custard at the edges of the container just begins to look melty, 10 to 15 minutes. Meanwhile, chop the chocolate-covered pretzels into rough 1/4-inch (6 1/4-millimeter) pieces (you should have about 2/3 cup).

Scoop the custard into a bowl, add the chopped chocolate-covered pretzels, and mix with a wooden spoon or spatula until the pretzels are well distributed in the custard. Scoop into two chilled bowls or cups, and serve at once.

Cinnamon-Granola Concrete

When I start making concretes, everything in the kitchen cabinet becomes fair game as a mix-in. I've tried nuts, dried fruit, chopped chocolate, about a dozen kinds of cookies, graham crackers, a piece of birthday cake, stale croissants, leftover cinnamon buns, and a few kinds of cereal. I've learned that the best mix-ins are hearty, a bit chewy, and offer a distinct textural contrast to the smooth, luxurious custard. Warmly spiced granola offers all that, and comes in so many flavors that you'll be mixing concretes for weeks.

2 cups vanilla frozen custard (about 16 ounces/454 grams)

½ teaspoon cinnamon

⅔ cup granola, flavor of your choice (about 4 ounces/112 grams)

MAKES ABOUT 2½ CUPS | 20 OUNCES | 600 MILLILITERS

Remove the frozen custard from the freezer and allow it to rest at room temperature until the custard at the edges of the container just begins to look melty, 10 to 15 minutes. Scoop the custard into a bowl, add the cinnamon and granola, and mix with a wooden spoon or spatula until the granola is well distributed in the custard. Scoop into two chilled bowls or cups, and serve at once.

Peanut-Molasses Shake

First manufactured in 1914 and still in production today, Mary Jane candies are the peanut butter- and molasses-flavored chews that inspired this shake. And they are from my own backyard.

Mary Janes are made by the New England Confectionery Company (NECCO for short, of NECCO Wafer fame), which until recently was located about three miles from my house. Even now, they're just a few towns over—about ten miles is all. With that kind of close proximity, I can eat Mary Janes and not blow my locavore aspirations.

½ cup cold whole or lowfat milk (about 4 ounces/125 milliliters)

3 tablespoons smooth peanut butter, preferably natural (about 1½ ounces/43 grams)

3 tablespoons molasses (about 2½ ounces/66 grams)

Pinch of salt

8 medium scoops French vanilla ice cream (about 1 quart/24 ounces/ 680 grams), softened until just melty at the edges

MAKES ABOUT 3½ CUPS | 28 OUNCES | 850 MILLILITERS

Place the milk, peanut butter, molasses, and salt in a blender and blend to mix thoroughly, about 30 seconds. Add the ice cream and pulse several times to begin breaking it up. With the blender motor off, use a flexible spatula to mash the mixture down onto the blender blades. Continue pulsing, stopping, and mashing until the mixture is well blended, thick, and moves easily in the blender jar, roughly 30 to 90 seconds. Pour into a chilled glass or glasses, and serve at once.

Facing page: Peanut-Molasses Shake.

Malted Orange-Molasses Shake

If you crave a full-flavor-forward shake, this fits the bill with the bittersweet intensity of molasses and a powerful hit of orange. Pure orange oil is the agent of that flavor, and pure citrus oils are incredibly potent, like the rocket fuel of the citrus world. So don't be tempted to splash in a bunch of orange oil here; a little dab really will do you. Look for orange oil along with other flavorings and extracts at the supermarket, gourmet shop, or online at www.boyajianinc.com or www.kalustyans.com. The distinct, slightly toasty flavor of malt rounds out the other two power player flavors.

½ cup cold whole or lowfat milk (about 4 ounces/125 milliliters)

3 tablespoons molasses (about 2 ½ ounces/66 grams)

¼ teaspoon pure orange oil

2 tablespoons malted milk powder (about 1 ounce/28 grams)

8 medium scoops caramel, caramel swirl, or dulce de leche ice cream (about 1 quart/24 ounces/ 680 grams), softened until just melty at the edges

MAKES ABOUT 3½ CUPS | 28 OUNCES | 850 MILLILITERS

Place the milk, molasses, orange oil, and malted milk powder in a blender and blend to mix thoroughly, about 30 seconds. Add the ice cream and pulse several times to begin breaking it up. With the blender motor off, use a flexible spatula to mash the mixture down onto the blender blades. Continue pulsing, stopping, and mashing until the mixture is well blended, thick, and moves easily in the blender jar, roughly 30 to 90 seconds. Pour into a chilled glass or glasses, and serve at once.

Marron Glacé Shake

Fall and winter is the time of year when Parisian *confiserie* windows burst with candied chestnuts, *marrons glacés* in French. To become glacé, the marrons go through a painstakingly long, labor-intensive process that culminates in forty-eight hours of poaching in a vanilla-laced sugar syrup. The finished confections are candied to their very core before being glazed and covered with individual foil wrappers.

Some of the luckiest marrons glacés are soaked in cognac to become *marrons glacés au cognac*, which are even more of a delicacy for the spiritually inclined among us. In fact, the chestnuts' flavor is so mild on its own that I found a little bit of cognac really amplifies it in the shake. A little bit more balances it, and becomes a variation (see next page.)

To flavor the shake I opt for less expensive, easier to find *crème de marron*, a sweetened chestnut puree. It should be available at upscale supermarkets and gourmet stores, or you can find it at www.kalustyans.com or www.markys.com. A small dollop of whipped cream and a few slivers of marron glacé make an elegant garnish.

(Recipe on next page)

½ cup cold whole or lowfat milk (about 4 ounces/125 milliliters)

½ cup crème de marron (about 5 ½ ounces/156 grams)

1 tablespoon cognac or brandy (about ½ ounce/15 milliliters)

¼ teaspoon pure vanilla extract

8 medium scoops French vanilla ice cream (about 1 quart/24 ounces/ 680 grams), softened until just melty at the edges

Place the milk, crème de marron, cognac, and vanilla extract in a blender and blend to mix thoroughly, about 30 seconds. Add the ice cream and pulse several times to begin breaking it up. With the blender motor off, use a flexible spatula to mash the mixture down onto the blender blades. Continue pulsing, stopping, and mashing until the mixture is well blended, thick, and moves easily in the blender jar, roughly 30 to 90 seconds. Pour into a chilled glass or glasses, and serve at once.

Marron Glacé au Cognac Variation

Follow the recipe for the Marron Glacé Shake, increasing the amount of cognac to 2 tablespoons (about 1 ounce/30 milliliters).

Tarte Tatin Shake

I honed my mania for all things apple with help from a true master, my sister Amanda. Never have I encountered someone who loves apples, in any way, shape, or form, as much as she. So it's no surprise that this appley, caramel-laced shake was her idea.

Get to know tarte Tatin, a buttery, deeply caramelized apple tart, if you don't already. There are hundreds of recipes around, it's got a great story, and it is one of the most romantically rustic French desserts there is. By most accounts, the tart was a cooking accident in the kitchen at the Hotel Tatin, run by the two Tatin sisters in the Loire Valley in the late nineteenth century. One sister was preparing an apple tart and mistakenly allowed the apples to cook too long in the butter and sugar. She draped pastry over the "ruined" apples and baked them anyway. To her surprise, the dinner guests loved the caramel-apple tart, and a classic was born.

Plain cider didn't provide enough applitude, so we reduced some to concentrate the flavor and added that as well. When you cool the reduced cider, it firms up to a jelly consistency because of the pectin in the apples. It will break down again in the blender. If you don't use the leftover reduced cider to make more shakes, try some spread on toast, pancakes, or a slice of plain pound cake. It also makes a great glaze for a pork roast or chops. Covered with plastic wrap, it will keep in the fridge for up to five days.

A tiny bit of Calvados, which is French apple brandy, intensifies the apple flavor further. A few thin slices of apple, sautéed quickly in butter and a little sugar until golden, would be a fitting garnish. (See photograph on page 151.)

(Recipe on next page)

2 ¼ cups apple cider, preferably unfiltered (about 18 ounces/550 milliliters)

2 teaspoons Calvados or apple brandy

Pinch of salt

4 medium scoops French vanilla ice cream (about 1 pint/ 12 ounces/340 grams), softened until just melty at the edges

4 medium scoops caramel, caramel swirl, or dulce de leche ice cream (about 1 pint/ 12 ounces/340 grams), softened until just melty at the edges

For the cider syrup Bring 2 cups (16 ounces/ 490 milliliters) of the cider to a boil in a medium saucepan over high heat; continue boiling until the liquid is reduced to about ¼ cup (2 ounces/60 milliliters), about 16 minutes. Cool to room temperature.

For the shake Place 2 tablespoons of the reduced cider, the remaining ¼ cup (2 ounces/60 milliliters) plain cider, the Calvados, and salt in a blender and blend to mix well, about 15 seconds. Add the ice cream and pulse several times to begin breaking it up. With the blender motor off, use a flexible spatula to mash the mixture down onto the blender blades. Continue pulsing, stopping, and mashing until the mixture is well blended, thick, and moves easily in the blender jar, roughly 30 to 90 seconds. Pour into a chilled glass or glasses, and serve at once.

Tarte Tatin au Calvados Variation

Follow the recipe for the Tarte Tatin Shake, increasing the amount of Calvados to 3 tablespoons (about 1½ ounces/45 milliliters).

Pain d'Épices Shake

A specialty of the Burgundy region in France, *pain d'épices*, which translates to "spice bread," is like gingerbread with more muscle. It's customary to use some rye flour along with the wheat, so while not at all tough, the texture (of a loaf or a slab, as opposed to soft or crunchy cookies, which are also common) is moist and on the dense side, right between cake and bread. As for flavor, a big dose of honey shares billing with warm spices, and often some type of orange flavoring as well. It was my slightly *pain d'épices*–obsessed sister Amanda's notion to translate this into a shake. I believe her exact words were: "Ohhhhh, Christmas in a glass!"

Orange oil is a very strong flavoring, so use it sparingly. If you can't find it in the supermarket or gourmet shop, try online at www.boyajianinc.com or www.kalustyans.com.

1/4 cup honey, preferably dark (about 3 ounces/85 grams)

1/8 teaspoon pure orange oil

1/2 teaspoon ground cinnamon

1/2 teaspoon freshly and finely ground black pepper

1/4 teaspoon ground cloves

1/4 teaspoon ground anise

1/8 teaspoon freshly grated nutmeg

1/2 cup cold whole or lowfat milk (about 4 ounces/125 milliliters)

8 medium scoops French vanilla ice cream (about 1 quart/24 ounces/ 680 grams), softened until just melty at the edges

MAKES ABOUT 3 1/2 CUPS | 28 OUNCES | 850 MILLILITERS

Stir together the honey, orange oil, cinnamon, pepper, cloves, anise, and nutmeg in a small microwavable bowl and microwave just until the honey is fluid and fragrant, 10 to 15 seconds; cool to room temperature. Place the spiced honey and the milk in a blender and blend to mix thoroughly, about 30 seconds. Add the ice cream and pulse several times to begin breaking it up. With the blender motor off, use a flexible spatula to mash the mixture down onto the blender blades. Continue pulsing, stopping, and mashing until the mixture is well blended, thick, and moves easily in the blender jar, roughly 30 to 90 seconds. Pour into a chilled glass or glasses, and serve at once.

Toasted Oatmeal and Brown Sugar Shake

This shake is the brainchild of my friend Dawn, who was inspired by the wide range of oatmeal-based drinks throughout Latin America and much of the Caribbean. In different countries the drinks may have different names—*chicha de avena* in Ecuador, *horchata de avena* in Guatemala, or *jugo de avena* (when it is mixed with juice) in the Dominican Republic—but the word *avena*, which is oatmeal in Spanish, is always present. In fact, the drinks are sometimes called just *avena*.

High-quality oats are essential here—keep the quick-cooking and instant "just-add-boiling-water" varieties in the cupboard. Bob's Red Mill, an Oregon company whose products are widely available, produces very good thick-cut rolled oats. They're also available online, at www.bobsredmill.com.

To make this shake with Scotch and honey, substitute 2 tablespoons (about 1 ounce/30 milliliters) Scotch whiskey for 2 tablespoons of the ½ cup milk in the shake, reduce the brown sugar to 2 tablespoons (about 1 ounce/36 grams), and add 2 tablespoons of honey (about 1 ½ ounces/43 grams) to the blender along with the ice cream.

(Recipe on next page)

Facing page: Toasted Oatmeal and Brown Sugar Shake.

1 tablespoon unsalted
butter (about
1/2 ounce/15 grams)

1/4 cup high-quality
rolled oats, preferably
thick cut (about
1 ounce/28 grams)

2/3 cup plus 1/2 cup cold
whole or lowfat milk
(about 9 ounces/
275 milliliters total)

2/3 cup water (about
5 ounces/150 milliliters)

Pinch of salt

3 tablespoons light
brown sugar (about
1 1/2 ounces/36 grams)

Pinch of ground cloves

8 medium scoops
French vanilla ice
cream (about
1 quart/24 ounces/
680 grams), softened
until just melty
at the edges

MAKES ABOUT 3 1/2 CUPS | 28 OUNCES | 850 MILLILITERS

For the oats Melt the butter in a small non-stick saucepan over medium heat until it stops foaming. Add the oats and cook, stirring constantly, until medium golden brown and fragrant, about 6 minutes. Standing back because the mixture will spit and sputter, add 2/3 cup milk, the water, and salt and bring to a boil. Reduce the heat to medium-low and simmer, stirring occasionally, until the oats are very soft and almost all of the liquid has been absorbed, about 18 minutes. Off the heat, cool the mixture to room temperature, about 20 minutes.

For the shake Place 1/2 cup (5 ounces/142 grams) of the cooked oats, the remaining 1/2 cup (4 ounces/125 milliliters) milk, the brown sugar, and cloves in a blender and blend until the oats are completely broken down and incorporated into the milk, about 1 1/2 minutes. Add the ice cream and pulse several times to begin breaking it up. With the blender motor off, use a flexible spatula to mash the mixture down onto the blender blades. Continue pulsing, stopping, and mashing until the mixture is well blended, thick, and moves easily in the blender jar, roughly 30 to 90 seconds. Pour into a chilled glass or glasses, and serve at once.

Maple-Bacon Shake

You heard me right—bacon. Not much . . . just enough to give this shake a faint but alluring savory note. A tiny pinch of salt focuses both the sweet and savory faces of this shake.

2 slices bacon (about 2 ounces/57 grams), cut into thin strips

6 tablespoons cold whole or lowfat milk (about 3 ounces/ 90 milliliters)

2 tablespoons pure maple syrup, preferably grade B (about 1 ounce/30 milliliters)

Pinch of salt

8 medium scoops French vanilla ice cream (about 1 quart/24 ounces/ 680 grams), softened until just melty at the edges

MAKES ABOUT 3½ CUPS | 28 OUNCES | 850 MILLILITERS

Fry the bacon in a small skillet set over medium heat, stirring frequently, until rendered and crisp, about 5 minutes. With a slotted spoon, remove the cooked bacon to paper towels to drain, and nibble on it or reserve it for another use. Off the heat, briefly cool the fat in the skillet.

Place the milk, maple syrup, 1 tablespoon of cooled bacon fat (if there is any more, you can discard it), salt, and ice cream in a blender and pulse several times to begin breaking up the ice cream. With the blender motor off, use a flexible spatula to mash the mixture down onto the blender blades. Continue pulsing, stopping, and mashing until the mixture is well blended, thick, and moves easily in the blender jar, roughly 30 to 90 seconds. Pour into a chilled glass or glasses, and serve at once.

Maple–Butter Pecan Shake

I have an abiding love for butter pecan ice cream, especially from Graeter's, a small, Ohio-based chain of ice cream parlors that originated in Cincinnati. Every time I visit Cincy, I try to make Graeter's my first stop on the way in, and my last on the way out. (You can also order the ice cream online at www.graeters.com).

The vanilla and caramel notes in real maple syrup (use dark grade B if you can, I think it's more flavorful than grade A) work beautifully with the butter-and-nut-flavored ice cream, so I added a bit.

Psssst . . . If need be, you can get away with using butter almond ice cream in place of the butter pecan. But you didn't hear that here.

½ cup cold whole or lowfat milk (about 4 ounces/125 milliliters)

½ cup chopped toasted pecans (about 2 ½ ounces/70 grams)

3 tablespoons pure maple syrup, preferably grade B (about 3 ounces/85 grams)

8 medium scoops butter pecan ice cream (about 1 quart/ 24 ounces/680 grams), softened until just melty at the edges

MAKES ABOUT 3 ½ CUPS | 28 OUNCES | 850 MILLILITERS

Place the milk, pecans, and maple syrup in a blender and blend to break down the pecans and mix thoroughly, about 30 seconds. Add the ice cream and pulse several times to begin breaking it up. With the blender motor off, use a flexible spatula to mash the mixture down onto the blender blades. Continue pulsing, stopping, and mashing until the mixture is well blended, thick, and moves easily in the blender jar, roughly 30 to 90 seconds. Pour into a chilled glass or glasses, and serve at once.

Facing page: Maple–Butter Pecan Shake.

Cold Buttered Rum Shake

I'm one of those people who always runs hot. Even in the dead of a Boston winter I rarely wear a heavy coat, and the temperature has to drop below freezing before I'll shut the windows all the way. Consequently, I'm not really one for hot drinks. It wouldn't even take all the fingers on one hand to count the mugs of hot buttered rum (the starting point for this shake, another brilliant idea from my sister Amanda) I've drunk in my lifetime.

Chill down those same flavors with some butter pecan ice cream, though, and I am on board! Rum and brown sugar, both with strong caramel notes, are natural partners for warm spices like clove and nutmeg, and in concert they play beautifully against the backdrop of a buttery-flavored ice cream.

¼ cup plus
1 tablespoon cold
whole or lowfat milk
(about 2 ½ ounces/
75 milliliters total)

3 tablespoons amber
or dark rum (about
1 ½ ounces/
45 milliliters)

3 tablespoons light
brown sugar (about
1 ½ ounces/36 grams)

Pinch of ground cloves

Pinch of freshly
grated nutmeg

8 medium scoops
butter pecan or butter
almond ice cream
(about 1 quart/
24 ounces/680 grams),
softened until just
melty at the edges

MAKES ABOUT 3 ½ CUPS | 28 OUNCES | 850 MILLILITERS

Place the milk, rum, brown sugar, cloves, and nutmeg in a blender and blend to mix thoroughly, about 15 seconds. Add the ice cream and pulse several times to begin breaking it up. With the blender motor off, use a flexible spatula to mash the mixture down onto the blender blades. Continue pulsing, stopping, and mashing until the mixture is well blended, thick, and moves easily in the blender jar, roughly 30 to 90 seconds. Pour into a chilled glass or glasses, and serve at once.

Orange Blossom and Honey Shake

Orange blossom water captures the essence of—what else?—orange blossoms. The scent and flavor are very, very sweet and floral, with faint citrus notes running through the background. Use it as you would rose water, just a tiny bit at a time, because it's very, very perfumy. You can buy orange blossom water, which is also called orange flower water, anywhere you can buy rose water, such as in Middle Eastern markets, or online at www.kalustyans.com.

6 tablespoons frozen orange juice concentrate, thawed (about 3 ounces/ 90 milliliters)

½ teaspoon orange blossom water

1½ tablespoons honey (about 1¼ ounces/32 grams)

8 medium scoops vanilla bean or original vanilla ice cream (about 1 quart/24 ounces/ 680 grams), softened until just melty at the edges

MAKES ABOUT 3½ CUPS | 28 OUNCES | 850 MILLILITERS

Place the orange juice concentrate, orange blossom water, and honey in a blender and blend to mix thoroughly, about 15 seconds. Add the ice cream and pulse several times to begin breaking it up. With the blender motor off, use a flexible spatula to mash the mixture down onto the blender blades. Continue pulsing, stopping, and mashing until the mixture is well blended, thick, and moves easily in the blender jar, roughly 30 to 90 seconds. Pour into a chilled glass or glasses, and serve at once.

Malted Caramel Shake

Okay, I'll admit it. When push comes to shove, I'm not really a caramel guy. I know I'm in the minority, though, because most people just love the stuff. In fact, as I talked up this book to my friends, I stopped counting the number of them who said, "Ohh, you'd better have a caramel shake in there."

So here it is, caramel lovers. I kept things easy by using caramel ice cream, rather than asking you to make homemade caramel, and I spiced things up a bit by adding malt, which, like the caramel itself, is a soft, sweet, mellow flavor. Food stylist Michael Pederson, clearly a caramel lover himself, thought that no caramel shake would be complete without a cap of whipped cream and drizzle of caramel sauce; you may want to follow in Michael's footsteps here.

½ cup cold whole or lowfat milk (about 4 ounces/125 milliliters)

¼ teaspoon pure vanilla extract

1 tablespoon malted milk powder (about ½ ounce/15 grams)

8 medium scoops caramel, caramel swirl, or dulce de leche ice cream (about 1 quart/24 ounces/680 grams), softened until just melty at the edges

MAKES ABOUT 3½ CUPS | 28 OUNCES | 850 MILLILITERS

Place the milk, vanilla extract, and malted milk powder in a blender and blend to mix thoroughly, about 15 seconds. Add the ice cream and pulse several times to begin breaking it up. With the blender motor off, use a flexible spatula to mash the mixture down onto the blender blades. Continue pulsing, stopping, and mashing until the mixture is well blended, thick, and moves easily in the blender jar, roughly 30 to 90 seconds. Pour into a chilled glass or glasses, and serve at once.

Facing page: Malted Caramel Shake.

SHAKES
(AND OTHER FROSTY FAVORITES)
FROM AFAR

Cholado

Cholados come from Colombia, but I encountered them first in the Latino neighborhood of Jackson Heights, Queens, in New York City. There is no ice cream involved, so a *cholado* isn't a shake, per se. With distinct fruity, icy, and creamy elements, you might think of it as fruit salad meets Slurpee meets melted sherbet. Eat the fruit with a spoon, and by the time you're done, the ice will have melted and blended with the syrup and milk. The mixture will be ice cold and thick, yet liquidy enough to slurp through a straw.

Within the basic formula of ice, syrup, fruit, and sweetened condensed milk, vary the syrup flavor and types of fruit however you wish. In my Jackson Heights experience, tropical fruits, cantaloupe, and strawberries were popular. Dynamic Health Laboratories (www.dynamichealth.com), Goya (www.goya.com), and Dafruta (www.wegmans.com) all make fruit concentrates that are great for *cholados*. You can even use thawed frozen orange juice concentrate, or your favorite fruit-flavored sorbet (I like raspberry, passion fruit, mango, or tangerine) in place of the syrup.

By the way, every *cholado* I've ever had was served in a plastic cup, so there is no need to get fancy with your glassware here. The standard garnish is a maraschino cherry and wafer sandwich cookie.

(Recipe on next page)

Facing page: Cholado.

3 cups shaved or crushed ice (about 20 ounces/568 grams)

6 tablespoons fruit concentrate or syrup, flavor of your choice (about 3 ounces/ 90 milliliters), or partially thawed frozen orange juice concentrate (about 3 ounces/90 milliliters), or 2 medium scoops sorbet, fruit flavor of your choice (about 1/2 pint/6 ounces/ 170 grams)

1/2 cup regular or lowfat sweetened condensed milk (about 4 ounces/125 milliliters)

2 cups mixed, cut fresh fruit, such as sliced banana or strawberries, halved grapes, and finely diced mango, papaya, pineapple, cantaloupe, peach, or nectarine (about 16 ounces/454 grams)

3 tablespoons shredded coconut

2 maraschino cherries

2 filled wafer cookies, for garnish, optional

Place 1½ cups (10 ounces/284 grams) of ice into each of two glasses. In each glass, top the ice with 3 tablespoons (1½ ounces/45 milliliters) fruit syrup or orange juice concentrate, or 1 scoop (¼ pint/3 ounces/85 grams) of sorbet, 3 tablespoons (1½ ounces/45 milliliters) sweetened condensed milk, and 1 cup (8 ounces/227 grams) of fruit (it's okay to mound the fruit above the rims of the glasses). Top the fruit in each glass with 1 tablespoon (½ ounce/15 milliliters) sweetened condensed milk, 1½ tablespoons coconut, a cherry, and a cookie, if using, and serve at once with a spoon, a straw, and lots of napkins.

Batidos

Simple fruit shakes called *batidos* (or *malteadas,* depending on the area) are wildly popular throughout the Caribbean and Central America, where fresh fruit is gorgeous and plentiful. Any ripe melon, berries, or tropical fruits soft enough to puree will make a great *batido.* The most basic *batidos* blend fresh fruit, ice, and milk, though it is very common to add some sweetener (usually sugar, sometimes honey), or a squirt of lime juice. Substituting or supplementing the milk with a small amount of sweetened condensed milk, or even cold water, is also common. I take a basic approach—fruit, ice, milk, and a small amount of sugar, if it's needed—so the *batido* comes out substantially lighter than an American shake. That said, a scoop or two of your favorite fruit sorbet makes a fine, if unorthodox, addition.

These recipes are easily halved. Or, if you have leftovers from a full batch, they'll keep overnight in a covered container in the fridge (longer than that and both the flavor and refreshment value fade). Shake the leftovers well to re-blend before serving.

Strawberry-Banana-Orange Batido

Depending on how sweet the berries are to start, you may want more or less sugar here. In the background, the bananas provide their trademark tropical sweetness, while the orange juice offers just enough acidity to tie the other flavors together and make them sing.

3 ½ cups sliced fresh or partially thawed frozen strawberries (about 28 ounces/794 grams)

¼ cup sugar (about 2 ounces/48 grams)

1 ½ cups ice cubes (about 6 large cubes/ 6 ounces/170 grams)

½ cup cold whole or lowfat milk (about 4 ounces/125 milliliters)

¼ cup frozen orange juice concentrate, partially thawed (about 2 ounces/60 milliliters)

1 medium, ripe banana, sliced (about 6 ounces/170 grams)

MAKES ABOUT 4½ CUPS | 36 OUNCES | 1¼ LITERS

Mix the strawberries and sugar in a medium nonreactive bowl and set aside until the strawberries begin to release some juices, about 10 minutes. Place the ice in the blender and pulse to crush the ice. Add the milk, orange juice concentrate, banana, and the strawberry mixture and pulse several times to begin breaking up the fruit. With the blender motor off, use a flexible spatula to mash the mixture down onto the blender blades. Continue pulsing, stopping, and mashing until the mixture is well blended, thick, and moves easily in the blender jar, roughly 30 to 90 seconds. Pour into a chilled glass or glasses, and serve at once.

Peach–Passion Fruit–Ginger Batido

Peach is not necessarily an authentic *batido* flavor, but don't let that deter you, because it makes a velvety smooth and luscious shake, with the requisite tropical note from the passion fruit and the clear, sweet snap of fresh ginger. If you don't have any passion fruit concentrate, you can substitute 3 scoops (about ¾ pint/9 ounces/255 grams) of passion fruit sorbet (which will increase the yield), or you can skip the passion fruit altogether and go with ½ cup (about 3 ounces/85 grams) of chopped fresh, ripe mango.

1 tablespoon grated or minced fresh ginger

¼ cup sugar (about 2 ounces/48 grams)

3 large, ripe peaches, peeled if desired, or 4 cups frozen sliced peaches, partially thawed (about 20 ounces/567 grams)

1 ½ cups ice cubes (about 6 large cubes/ 6 ounces/170 grams)

½ cup cold whole or lowfat milk (about 4 ounces/125 milliliters)

¼ cup passion fruit concentrate or syrup (about 2 ounces/ 60 milliliters) or ½ cup chopped fresh, ripe mango (about 3 ounces/85 grams)

1 tablespoon freshly squeezed lime juice (about ½ ounce/ 15 milliliters)

MAKES ABOUT 4½ CUPS | 36 OUNCES | 1¼ LITERS

Place the ginger and sugar in a medium nonreactive bowl and stir until the sugar is moist and fragrant. Add the peaches, toss to coat them with the sugar, and set aside until they begin to release some juices, about 10 minutes. Place the ice in the blender and pulse to crush the ice. Add the milk, passion fruit concentrate, lime juice, and peach mixture and pulse several times to begin breaking up the fruit. With the blender motor off, use a flexible spatula to mash the mixture down onto the blender blades. Continue pulsing, stopping, and mashing until the mixture is well blended, thick, and moves easily in the blender jar, roughly 30 to 90 seconds. Pour into a chilled glass or glasses, and serve at once.

Licuados

In Mexico, *batidos* are called *licuados*. When you order a *licuado*, you are generally given the choice of *con agua*, which means "with water," or *con leche*—"with milk," and *con jugo*, meaning "with juice" (usually orange), is not unheard of. The vendor will also probably ask if you want *azucar*, or "sugar." I prefer *con agua, azucar y limon*—water, sugar, and lime. Just as with a *batido*, any ripe, soft fruit works well for *licuados*.

These recipes are easily halved. Or, if you have leftovers from a full batch, they'll keep overnight in a covered container in the fridge (longer than that and both the flavor and refreshment value fade). Shake the leftovers well to re-blend before serving.

Pineapple Licuado

Wherever I've been in Mexico, small shops and street vendors selling fresh cut fruit, *licuados*, and *aguas frescas* (see page 187) are a dime a dozen. Though I have never met a *licuado* that I didn't like, I always go for pineapple if it's available because I love the way it is at once both sweet and bracing, like a tropical wake-up call. Most supermarkets now sell cut fresh pineapple, which is an irresistible shortcut.

1 ½ cups ice cubes (about 6 large cubes/ 6 ounces/170 grams)

½ cup very cold water (about 4 ounces/ 125 milliliters)

1 tablespoon freshly squeezed lime juice (about ½ ounce/ 15 milliliters)

4 cups cold, ripe, 1 ½-inch pineapple chunks (about 24 ounces/680 grams)

6 tablespoons sugar (3 ounces/72 grams)

MAKES ABOUT 4½ CUPS | 36 OUNCES | 1¼ LITERS

Place the ice in the blender and pulse to crush. Place the water, lime juice, pineapple, and sugar in the blender and pulse several times to begin breaking up the fruit. With the blender motor off, use a flexible spatula to mash the mixture down onto the blender blades. Continue pulsing, stopping, and mashing until the mixture is well blended, thick, and moves easily in the blender jar, roughly 30 to 90 seconds. Pour into a chilled glass or glasses, and serve at once.

Pineapple-Mint Variation

Follow the recipe for the Pineapple Licuado, adding ¼ cup (about ½ ounce/15 grams) of chopped fresh mint to the blender along with the water, lime juice, pineapple, and sugar.

Blueberry-Honeydew Licuado

Melon is very common in *licuados*, and with good reason. Honeydew and cantaloupe both possess such interesting flavors—sweet to be sure, but with faint vegetable notes in the background. And when they are chilled and blended with ice, there is nothing more refreshing. Blueberries boost the melon flavor without masking it; they also add color, and if such things concern you, healthy antioxidants, as well.

1 1/2 cups ice cubes (about 6 large cubes/ 6 ounces/170 grams)

1/2 cup very cold water (about 4 ounces/125 milliliters)

1 1/2 tablespoons freshly squeezed lime juice (about 3/4 ounce/25 milliliters)

3 1/2 cups cold, ripe, 1 1/2-inch (4-centimeter) honeydew chunks (about 24 ounces/ 680 grams)

1/2 cup fresh or thawed frozen blueberries (about 3 ounces/85 grams)

2 tablespoons sugar (1 ounce/24 grams)

MAKES ABOUT 4 1/2 CUPS | 36 OUNCES | 1 1/4 LITERS

Place the ice in the blender and pulse to crush the ice. Add the water, lime juice, honeydew, blueberries, and sugar and pulse several times to begin breaking up the fruit. With the blender motor off, use a flexible spatula to mash the mixture down onto the blender blades. Continue pulsing, stopping, and mashing until the mixture is well blended, thick, and moves easily in the blender jar, roughly 30 to 90 seconds. Pour into a chilled glass or glasses, and serve at once.

Aguas Frescas

Agua fresca, which translates literally to "fresh water," is even lighter in consistency than the *licuado* because it generally contains a higher ratio of water to fruit. Sometimes called *agua fruta* ("fruit water"), it really is meant to be a beverage—ice cold liquid refreshment for hot, hot Mexican days. The *aguas frescas* I have ordered in Mexico have been surprisingly and delightfully mild in flavor—the perfect foil for spicy Mexican food.

The stands where *aguas frescas* are sold often display huge jars of *aguas* in different colors—scarlet red strawberry and hibiscus (called Jamaica), pink watermelon, pale orange cantaloupe, faint green lime, brown tamarind, and vibrant yellow pineapple. Luminescent white *horchata*, a Mexican drink made from rice, almonds, cinnamon, and sugar, is also available at the stands.

Depending on the vendor, the *aguas* may or may not be served with ice; the purists I've queried agree that ice is undesirable because it dilutes an already mild drink. I forgo the ice, but do use ice cold water and well chilled fruit, and I chill the *agua* for as long as possible before serving it. Watermelon, or *sandia* in Spanish, is far and away my favorite flavor for *agua fresca*.

These recipes are easily halved. Or, if you have leftovers from a full batch, they'll keep in a covered container in the fridge for a couple of days. Stir the leftover *agua* well to re-blend before serving.

Watermelon Agua Fresca

This *agua* will convince you that seedless watermelon is the greatest thing since sliced bread. Don't despair if your watermelon does have seeds, though, because in Mexico they usually don't bother removing them—the seeds are ground right into the drink, and they settle quickly to the bottom of the container. My *agua* is a little heavier on the fruit than many I've tried in Mexico because I like the stronger flavor. That doesn't seem to detract from its refreshment value—at barbecues and parties pitchers of it go as fast as I put them out.

1 cup very cold water (about 8 ounces/ 250 milliliters)

4 cups cold, ripe, 1½-inch (4-centimeter) watermelon chunks, preferably seedless (about 24 ounces/680 grams)

1 tablespoon freshly squeezed lime juice (about ½ ounce/ 15 milliliters)

Pinch of salt

1½ tablespoons sugar, or to taste, optional (about ¾ ounce/18 grams)

MAKES ABOUT 4 CUPS | 32 OUNCES | 1 LITER

Place the water, watermelon, lime juice, salt, and sugar, if using, in a blender and puree the fruit well, roughly 30 seconds. Taste the *agua* and correct the seasoning with additional lime juice or sugar if desired, pour into a pitcher, and chill for at least 1 hour. Just before serving, stir the *agua* to blend, pour into a chilled glass or glasses, and serve at once.

Watermelon-Cucumber Variation

Follow the recipe for the Watermelon Agua Fresca, replacing 1 cup of the watermelon cubes with three-quarters of a medium cucumber (about 6 ounces/170 grams), peeled, seeded, and roughly chopped.

Facing page: Watermelon Agua Fresca.

Yogurt Drinks

Throughout Turkey, the Middle East, and India, yogurt is eaten—and drunk—on a daily basis. A component in countless dishes throughout these regions, yogurt is also the basis for salted drinks that go by different names, depending on the country. For instance, the same basic mixture of yogurt, water, and salt is known as *laban* or *laban ayran* in Syria and Lebanon, *laban arbil* in Iraq, and *shenina* in Jordan.

Turkish *ayran* is a version with which Americans might be familiar. It is a streamlined drink—simply yogurt beaten with plain or sparkling water, and seasoned with a pinch of salt. Sometimes a pinch of sugar and fresh or dried mint are added as well. Proportions of yogurt to water depend on how thick a drink you want in the end (the baseline consistency is like whole milk), as well as on the thickness of the yogurt with which you start.

In the United States, the undisputed king of yogurt-based shakes is the Indian *lassi*. As is the case with any type of shake, there are as many individual recipes as there are cooks. Broadly speaking though, *lassis* fall into two general categories: salted or sweet. Both are intended to be drunk ice cold, to provide relief from the heat and humidity. Salted *lassis* are very often flavored with cumin, chile, and/or dried mint, and always, as the name indicates, salt.

In my book, sweet *lassis* are easier to love than their salted brethren. Sweet *lassis* are frequently flavored with rose water, mint, or cardamom, or a combination, as well as with fruits including mangoes, strawberries, lychees, and bananas. Of these, mango is probably the most popular, and certainly the most familiar *lassi* in our part of the world.

Following are basic recipes for salted *lassi*, sweet *lassi*, and mango *lassi*, as well as for a Turkish *ayran*. These recipes are easily halved. Or, if you have leftovers from a full batch, they'll keep overnight in a covered container in the fridge (longer than that and both the flavor and refreshment value fade). Shake the leftovers well to re-blend before serving.

On the topic of yogurt, I much prefer the whole-milk and lowfat varieties to nonfat yogurt, which has a chalky feel in the mouth. Also, stick to plain, unflavored yogurt for all of the drinks in this section. To my taste, plain yogurt has the most tang for the buck.

Salted Lassi

Dried red chile flakes are often used to give salted *lassi* some spicy heat. I prefer minced fresh jalapeño instead, and I usually add a few seeds for extra thrust. You can use other hot chiles in place of the jalapeño, adjusting the quantity for the heat and your taste. You can also substitute an equal amount of cold water for the ice, in which case you can simply whisk the ingredients in a pitcher or bowl and forgo the blender.

1 1/2 cups ice cubes (about 6 large cubes/ 6 ounces/170 grams)

2 cups cold, plain, whole-milk or lowfat yogurt (about 16 ounces/454 grams)

1/2 teaspoon salt, or to taste

1/2 teaspoon ground cumin, or to taste

Finely ground black pepper, to taste, optional

1 1/2 teaspoons minced fresh jalapeño, with or without seeds, as desired

MAKES ABOUT 3 CUPS | 24 OUNCES | 750 MILLILITERS

Place the ice, yogurt, salt, cumin, black pepper if using, and jalapeño in a blender and blend until well blended and the mixture moves easily in the blender jar, roughly 45 seconds. Taste the *lassi* and correct the seasoning with additional salt, cumin, or black pepper, if desired. Pour into a chilled glass or glasses, and serve at once.

Minted Variation

Follow the recipe for the Salted Lassi, adding 3 tablespoons of chopped fresh mint to the blender along with the other ingredients.

Sweet Lassi

Unless you grew up drinking salted *lassis*, they are probably an acquired taste. Not so the sweet version, which delicately balances the tang of the yogurt with sugar. I add a small hit of aromatic cardamom, for good measure.

1 ½ cups ice cubes (about 6 large cubes/ 6 ounces/170 grams)

2 cups cold, plain, whole-milk or lowfat yogurt (about 16 ounces/454 grams)

3 tablespoons sugar, or to taste (about 1 ½ ounces/36 grams)

Pinch of salt

¼ teaspoon ground cardamom, or to taste

MAKES ABOUT 3 CUPS | 24 OUNCES | 750 MILLILITERS

Place the ice, yogurt, sugar, salt, and cardamom in a blender and blend until well blended and the mixture moves easily in the blender jar, roughly 45 seconds. Taste the *lassi* and correct the seasoning with additional sugar, salt, or cardamom, if desired. Pour into a chilled glass or glasses, and serve at once.

Mango Lassi

In the tropical and subtropical world, mangoes are a staple food. Of course they're widely available in North America, too, yet I still think of them as a vaguely exotic treat, with a flavor somewhere between peach and pineapple. Ripe mangoes give slightly to gentle pressure, like a ripe peach, and emit a floral, faintly sweet fragrance from the stem end. Pre-cut fresh or frozen mango chunks are a fine shortcut here.

1 ½ cups ice cubes (about 6 large cubes/ 6 ounces/170 grams)

1 ½ large ripe mangoes, peeled, pitted, flesh roughly chopped (about 2 cups/about 16 ounces/ 454 grams)

1 cup cold, plain, whole-milk or lowfat yogurt (about 8 ounces/227 grams)

3 tablespoons sugar, or to taste (about 1 ½ ounces/36 grams)

Pinch of salt

MAKES ABOUT 4 CUPS | 32 OUNCES | 1 LITER

Place the ice, mango, yogurt, sugar, and salt in a blender and blend until well blended and the mixture moves easily in the blender jar, roughly 45 seconds. Taste the *lassi* and correct the seasoning with additional sugar or salt, if desired. Pour into a chilled glass or glasses, and serve at once.

Ayran

Feel free to opt for still water in place of the sparkling. You are going for a milky consistency here.

2 cups cold sparkling water (about 16 ounces/500 milliliters)

2 cups cold, plain, whole-milk or lowfat yogurt (about 16 ounces/454 grams)

Pinch of salt

Ice cubes, for serving

MAKES ABOUT 4 CUPS | 32 OUNCES | 1 LITER

Whisk the sparkling water, yogurt, and salt in a medium bowl or pitcher until well blended. Taste the *ayran* and adjust the consistency with extra sparkling water or yogurt, if desired. Place a few ice cubes in one or two chilled glasses, pour in the ayran, and serve at once.

INDEX

Note: Page numbers in **boldface** type refer to recipes themselves; those in *italic* type refer to photographs.

ABOUT THE AUTHOR

Adam Ried is the cooking columnist for the Sunday *Boston Globe Magazine* and a contributor to *Cook's Country*, *Fine Cooking*, Hannaford *fresh*, and other publications. He is also the kitchen equipment specialist on both the top-rated PBS cooking show *America's Test Kitchen* and the new PBS series *Cook's Country from America's Test Kitchen*. As an editor for *Cook's Illustrated* Adam developed and edited recipes and feature stories and was responsible for the highly respected kitchen equipment testing and ingredient tasting programs and features. He lives in Cambridge, Massachusetts. His Web site is www.adamried.com.